BBC BOOKS

TopGear
THE COOL 500
THE COOLEST CARS EVER MADE

Matt Master

CONTENTS

INTRODUCTION

It's tricky to determine exactly when the notion of cool might first be applied to personal transport. Horses and camels don't really count on their own, not even the quick ones. A glance into the annals of A to B would suggest that there were some fairly nifty chariots knocking about in Ancient Rome. Fast ones, brightly coloured, attached to a proper thoroughbred, that sort of thing. But cool is, of course, a subjective concept, and entirely relative. Neolithic man probably felt quite special rubbing mammoth fat on to the first stone-age axle, just as the post war suburbanite found solace buffing the behind of his Austin A40.

So what earns any car a spot in this hallowed 500 depends on various factors, some of them indefinable. We start at the very beginning, give or take a few years, and chart the progress of the car's unpredictable and extraordinary evolution. You'll recognize many entries as deserved icons of our automotive age, and probably see a few you'd rather had been consigned to memory's scrapheap. But all, for some reason or another, are here because they're special. Not just things for getting around in, but things that make the very act of clambering aboard and turning the key an emotional and rewarding ritual. This, then, is the history of cars minus all the boring bits; *Top Gear*'s chronology of cool.,.

1900–1949
IN THE BEGINNING

You'll notice as we work our way through the 20th century that the post-war years get a decade to themselves, whereas the first half of the century has an unceremonious chunk. This you can blame on the relatively slow technological progress of the automobile. There weren't that many cars to get excited about in the first part of the 20th century, and those there were tend to look a bit samey. To make matters worse, if any photographs exist they usually look as if they were taken at night with a pinhole camera.

Nevertheless, the early 1900s was a significant period in the development of the car and did produce some jaw-droppers that are worthy rivals to the latest high-tech supercars.

We are all indebted to the pioneers, entrepreneurs, mad inventors and lunatic drivers who shoved the evolution of motoring into first gear and leant heavily on the accelerator. From horse to horsepower, this was a leap into the unknown that was to reshape society like nothing that had gone before...

Although by no means the first car, the Mercedes 35hp is widely regarded as the godfather of modern motoring. What had gone before tended to be a cart with an engine and a tiller where the horse was meant to be. These things were not built to go round corners with the sort of speeds that internal combustion made available and, in fact, were regularly found upside-down with any occupants scattered in the ditches.

So the head engineer at Daimler, a man called Wilhelm Maybach no less, took the pony and trap design back to the drawing board and effectively invented the car.

It was longer, wider and lower than anything else on the road, and had a bespoke chassis and lightweight steel bodywork. It also had a bigger and highly technical engine bolted directly to the chassis, lowering the centre of gravity and increasing stability.

The 35hp was built to go racing. Commissioned by a wealthy Austrian who named the car after his daughter, Mercedes, it would quickly become a dominant force in competition before being modified as a family car by simply adding two more seats. The success of the 35hp led to the Mercedes name being officially adopted by Daimler a year later. History was in the making.

28 June 1914

A rare 1910 Double Phaeton limousine built by the Austrian manufacturers Gräf & Stift escaped largely unscathed when Archduke Franz Ferdinand and his wife, Sophie, are shot dead in the back seat while visiting in Sarajevo.

1906 **Rolls-Royce Silver Ghost** ▼

In the early 20th century, reliability was not something the motorist took for granted. In fact the exact opposite was the case. Cars broke down all the time, abandoning you at the roadside to roll up your sleeves and try to fix them. Either that or to read the paper while your chauffeur got on with it. But in 1906 Rolls-Royce unveiled the 40/50 hp, quickly dubbed the Silver Ghost after the factory demonstrator was painted aluminium and bedecked in silver plate. The Silver Ghost proved that cars could be reliable, as well as fast, quiet and elegant. You could trust this car to get you wherever you needed to go, and to take you there in hushed and stately comfort. Small wonder then that the Silver Ghost was supplied to the royal family and hailed by the contemporary press as 'the best car in the world'.

In production for nearly 20 years, it was the Silver Ghost that cemented Rolls-Royce's reputation, and in doing so set the bar alarmingly high for all other manufacturers.

1908 **Ford Model T** ▲

This is the car universally credited with starting it all. Although the automobile had been available to the privileged few for almost a decade, 1908 was the year that motoring made it to the masses. The Model T was conceived by Henry Ford as the car for anyone and everyone. It was simple, versatile and easy to maintain. It was also the first car to be built on a moving assembly line, making it cost-effective to manufacture and therefore, crucially, affordable. Ten years on, around half the cars in the US were Model Ts and by the time production stopped in 1927, over 15 million had been made worldwide. There was nothing particularly cool about the T's appearance, or performance for that matter, but this was the car that invited the most of us to the party. And for that we are forever indebted.

1924 **Bugatti Type 35** ▼

The first Bugatti in our line up is, fittingly, an out-and-out racer. This car utterly dominated Grand Prix racing in the mid-20s, with its 2.0-litre, in-line, 8-cylinder engine more than a match for a lowly 750kg kerbweight. It is estimated that from 1924 until 1931 when the Type 35 ceased production, it racked up well over a thousand competition victories in the hands of works drivers and privateers, making it the most successful racing Bugatti ever made. A little over 200 were built, in both supercharged and normally aspirated forms, and the few surviving models today command eye-watering prices at auction. This is where it really began for Bugatti, and that front grille became a design hallmark that even made it on to the Veyron.

◀ 1925 **Rolls-Royce Phantom**

About the same time that Ettore Bugatti was building the lightweight 35 sports car, Rolls-Royce was busy banging together the vast and absurdly powerful Phantom. This was a luxury machine squarely targeted at the mega-rich. And every one was unique, for instead of labouring to the troublesome whims of its picky, aristocratic clientele, Rolls-Royce simply built the Phantom's chassis and mighty 8-litre engine and then left the customer to choose his own coachbuilder to design and fit a body.

One of the Phantom's peculiar claims to fame was the ability to accelerate from a crawl to top speed in a single gear, making the remaining three gears all but redundant, and the life of its chauffeur comparatively cushy.

1927 **Bugatti Type 41 Royale** ▼

Reputedly piqued by the growing renown of Rolls-Royce, Ettore Bugatti set out to build the definitive luxury car. Sawing a 16-cylinder aircraft engine in half, Ettore still had a 12.7-litre, straight-eight to play with, enough to make something substantially larger and more powerful than anything the British had previously dared dream of.

With all that space, unimaginable luxury was, of course, a shoo-in. But Ettore hadn't counted on the Great Depression, a worldwide recession so severe that even his extensive list of royal clientele were refusing their eagerly awaited orders at the point of delivery.

In the end only six Type 41s were ever made, and just three sold.

1928 **Bentley 4.5-Litre Supercharged** ▶

Against the wishes of owner Walter Owen Bentley, and funded in true Jeeves-and-Wooster style by the Honourable Dorothy Paget, a man called Henry Birkin set about supercharging a series of 4.5-litre Bentleys in order to take them racing.

Ettore Bugatti is famously quoted grumbling about "the fastest lorry in the world", and they were indeed staggeringly fast and powerful, particularly for cars of such a size and at such a time. But all that grunt didn't come without its problems. Despite leaving the field for dead in various outings, the Bentley 4.5-Litre Supercharged never won at Le Mans and was soon surpassed by the sturdier, larger-capacity Speed Six.

1928 **Invicta 4.5 Low Chassis S-Type** ▶

Although a comparative rarity against the Bentleys and Bugattis of the pre-war era, the Invicta is regarded by many a motoring connoisseur as a worthy rival, thanks to its obvious elegance and technical innovation.

The Invicta was a subtly styled and practical four-seater that concealed vast reserves of torque within its 4.5-litre Meadows engine.

The S-Type was capable of hitting 100mph, no mean feat for a road car in 1928, and saw inevitable competition success at Brooklands, and even on the Monte Carlo Rally.

1928 **Mercedes-Benz SSK** ▶

Despite an outward appearance suggestive of silk suits and fur coats, the SSK was, and still is, one of the great sports cars of all time. A top speed of 120mph made Merc's supercharged 7.1-litre, two-seat roadster the fastest car in the world, but its chopped-down wheelbase and lightweight materials also made it one of the most agile, with countless Grand Prix wins and the 1931 Mille Miglia (the Italian open-road race) soon under its belt. Designed by none other than Dr Ferdinand Porsche, just before he started his own little concern, this is one of mankind's definitive triumphs of form and function.

1929 **Bentley Speed Six**

One of the enduring images of pre-war British motoring is a chap (not just a man, mind) in goggles and leather helmet, clinging on for dear life to the enormous wooden steering wheel of a racing green Bentley. The car in question is invariably the Speed Six, a racing version of the 6.5-litre that had appeared two years before.

The Speed Six enjoyed back-to-back wins at Le Mans in 1929 and 1930, blowing the daintier competition from France and Italy into the weeds.

The winning driver in both years was Woolf Barnato, the man behind one of the great motoring stories of the age. At a party in Cannes, he claimed his Speed Six was so much faster than the Blue Train Express between Cannes and Calais that, if they departed Cannes together, he would be seated in his London club before the Blue Train had made the French port.

A sizeable wager was agreed and Barnato set off with a relief driver the following evening at the same time as the train. In terrible weather and on poor roads, the pair drove at breakneck speeds, arriving at their club in St James four minutes before the train pulled in to Calais.

This was to be Bentley's most successful racing car of all time and remains in many a dewy eye the epitome of British motoring might.

1931 Alfa Romeo 8C Tipo B Monoposto ▼

The 8C moniker, referring to an eight-cylinder engine, was applied to a bewildering number of Alfa Romeos throughout the 1930s. They included two-seat roadsters and competition coupés, luxurious larger road cars and the world's first single seat Grand Prix racer.

This, the 8C Tipo B Monoposto, is perhaps the most famous of all the 8Cs. Using the then fairly radical concept of twin superchargers and borrowing lightweight aluminium technology from the aviation industry, the Tipo B had an astonishing power-to-weight ratio. And with its single seat hung low between an ingenious split prop shaft, the Tipo B's handling was first class.

In the hands of racing legends Tazio Nuvolari and Rudolph Caracciola the Tipo B utterly dominated Grand Prix racing in the mid-30s. And even as the 8C became outgunned by more powerful German offerings from Mercedes-Benz and Auto Union, the little Alfa continued to win races thanks to its balance and agility. Quintessential Italian motoring.

1933 **Pierce-Arrow Silver Arrow** ▼

Pierce-Arrow was a New York-based manufacturer of exclusive but understated cars that found favour with Hollywood royalty and the East Coast aristocracy.

The Silver Arrow was its greatest product: unquestionably beautiful, comfortable, luxurious and powerful. Featuring a mighty 7.6-litre, V12 engine and an unusually streamlined fastback design that was one of the first beneficiaries of wind-tunnel testing, the Silver Arrow was significantly ahead of its time. But its time happened to fall in the darkest days of the Great Depression, a period when even the mega-rich wanted to avoid conspicuous acts of consumption. Intended as an attention-grabbing flagship for the marque, it was a masterstroke doomed to failure. Uptake was all but non-existent and in the end only five Silver Arrows were ever made.

◄ 1934 **Austin 7 EK75**

The Austin 7 was a small, sturdy and practical little runabout that did pretty much for Britain what the Model T did for the United States. Which is to say that almost everyone seemed to have one and nobody much cared to talk about it.

But for the greater part of its long lifetime, the humble 7 was meddled with by motorsports enthusiasts who saw the virtues of this simple and malleable machine. The EK75, aptly nicknamed the Speedy, was arguably the greatest exponent of such reinvention. Shod in lightweight aluminium and with an aerodynamic tail, it was capable of reaching speeds that would attract the attention of your local law enforcement today, and all this in a tiny tin-foil bath tub with not much in the way of brakes.

1934 **Citroën Traction Avant** ▶

In production for just short of 20 years, the Traction Avant – meaning front-wheel drive – was as much a part of the landscape of mid-20th century France as onion-laden bicycles and Panzer tanks.

It is estimated that over three-quarters of a million Avants were made and sold worldwide, with factories popping up as far afield as Copenhagen and, er, Slough.

Using a then radical monocoque (single-shell) chassis design with highly advanced front suspension, the Avant was light but strong and remarkably good to drive. On the inside, clever packaging also made it unusually spacious. In almost every way the Traction Avant was a real pioneer, setting countless design precedents that are still easily recognisable today.

1934 **Chrysler Airflow** ▼

Where the bold advances of the Citroën Traction Avant were embraced by an open-minded pre-war Europe, similar design and engineering efforts fell on stony ground across the pond. The Chrysler Airflow was also a radical product on quite a few levels, including near 50/50 weight distribution and a steel spaceframe construction, but the thing that really turned off a sceptical American market was the styling.

Using early wind-tunnel technology, the Airflow's highly streamlined aeronautical emphasis was too much for a national psyche seemingly resistant to change. Desperate attempts by Chrsyler to un-design the avant-garde Airflow failed to tempt back buyers and within three years it had disappeared.

1 June 1935

Car drivers are forced to take compulsory driving tests in Britain. Scarily, up until this point you didn't have to sit a test. Even more scarily, of the 246,000 who sit the simple new test, only 155,000 actually pass. Perhaps scariest of all, the first person to pass is a Mr Beene.

1935 **Aston Martin Ulster** ▼

The Ulsters were a series of high-performance road cars with tiny, 1.5-litre engines. This modest grunt was offset by lightweight aluminium bodywork and a high state of tune, meaning the Ulster would easily pass 100mph – none too shabby back then for a road-legal two-seater.

Built to ensure they complied with contemporary racing regulations, Aston then campaigned the Ulster to appreciable competition success before the war, finally winning its class and finishing third overall at Le Mans in 1935.

◄ 1936 **Cord 810**

Cord was a short-lived American manufacturer best known for the 810, an automotive beauty that deserved to do far better than history allows. Sharing innovation with Citroën's Traction Avant above, the 810 was America's first front-wheel-drive car, with independent front suspension. It also had a semi-automatic transmission and pop-up headlights, all of which caused a massive stir when the car was first unveiled in New York in 1935.

Orders came thick and fast, too fast for Cord, and when the first 810s reached customers in 1936 they were beset with reliability issues.

Early interest soon waned and by the following year, with the US economy still flailing, Cord in its entirety was mothballed.

1936 **SS 100 Jaguar** ▼

Had it not been for the Nazis, Jaguar may never have existed. Not a statement you're likely to read on their website, but it's true, sort of. For when SS Cars Ltd started building the 100 in Coventry in 1936 they hadn't banked on Hitler borrowing the SS monogram. After the war Swallow Sidecars became Jaguar and the 100, which had ceased production just as war began, was forever then referred to as the 'Jaguar SS 100.'

One of the classic pre-war shapes, the SS is that perfect blend of elegant understatement and sporting promise. And with a muscular straight-six lashed low beneath that long, louvred bonnet, it was capable of seeing off 100mph, the first affordable sportscar to do so.

Sadly, the war cut short both demand and supply and fewer than 200 were ever made.

1936 **Mercedes-Benz 540K** ▶

A development of the all-conquering SSK from a few years before, the Mercedes-Benz 540K seems to encapsulate all the aggression and intent of 1930s Nazi Germany. Massive, enormously powerful and highly technologically advanced, it was a brute of a thing and the polar opposite of the svelte and agile Jaguar SS above.

The 540K's 5.4-litre, straight-eight engine was supercharged to develop 180bhp, enough to haul it to around 110mph. But this was also made possible by the lightweight tubular chassis developed for Merc's Silver Arrows racers. The 540K ceased production in 1940, marking the end of a remarkable era for Mercedes-Benz. Things would never quite be the same.

1937 **Fiat 500 Topolino** ▶

The Topolino can lay claim to being the very first city car, although its duties as Italy's budget runabout were far more varied than that. Despite having a front-mounted, water-cooled four-cylinder engine, it was absolutely tiny and cheap as chips by the standards of the day.

Production continued right up until 1955 and in that time it's reckoned that over half a million Topolinos were made. It was eventually replaced by the more spacious air-cooled, rear engine Fiat 600 and 500, but neither quite had the charm of car Italy called the 'Little Mouse'.

1937 **Talbot-Lago T150 CSS** ▼

The T150 CSS is widely considered to be one the most beautiful cars in the world. And we're not going to argue.

In the late 1930s, the Paris-based Talbot-Lago began producing expensive, six-cylinder sports cars and racing them with some success.

With the help of coachbuilders Figoni and Falaschi, the touring coupé, designated T150 CSS, appeared, and jaws dropped around the world. Its extraordinary design was immediately referred to as the 'teardrop,' an ingenious blend of aesthetic and aerodynamic understanding. And as if to press home the point, a factory standard car, one of only fourteen ever made, was entered for Le Mans in 1938. It finished third.

1937 **Lancia Aprilia** ▶

The original Aprilia looks pretty humdrum amid these pages of excess and extravagance, but beneath that humble saloon bodywork lay some unprecedented technical advances that made it one of the original, and most unlikely, Q-cars – a real wolf in sheep's clothing. It had a light but rigid monocoque, independent suspension all round and an incredibly aerodynamic profile honed in wind tunnels. Using a compact but powerful 1.3-litre V4, the slick and supple Aprilia was capable of hitting 80mph, a shock to vastly more expensive and ostensibly sportier cars of the time.

1937 **Bugatti 57 SC Atlantic** ▶

Echoing the silhouette of the Talbot-Lago T150 coupé, Bugatti's now legendary 57 SC Atlantic appeared at a time when French car design was at its most bold and ingenious.

The prototype was made of an ultra-lightweight magnesium and aluminium alloy, but the former's flammability made building the car slightly hazardous, so the three official production cars reverted back to plain aluminium. These were all powered by 3.3-litre straight-eights which were retrospectively supercharged by the factory, enabling the Atlantic to hit astonishing speeds for the day.

Considered Bugatti's ultimate creation, an Atlantic recently changed hands for a record-breaking £20 million.

1938 **Alfa Romeo Alfetta 158** ▶

Small has always been beautiful in the minds of Italian race engineers, and the Alfetta (meaning Little Alfa) 158 was a masterclass in the art.

Alfa designed the 158 to take on the larger, heavier Grand Prix cars of the day with a tiny, 1.5-litre, eight-cylinder engine ultimately supercharged to over 300bhp. And in doing so they created one of the most dominant racing cars of all time.

On hold (and hidden) during the war, the Alfettas returned to competition as the all-new Formula One series began, and in 1950, a full twelve years after it was designed, the 158 won every single race it entered.

1938 **Mercedes-Benz W154 Silver Arrow** ▼

Built as a rapid response to Grand Prix rule changes, the Mercedes-Benz W154 is regarded as the pinnacle of supercharging in Germany's Silver Arrow arsenal. With a smaller V12 up front still nearing 500bhp at 8000 rpm, the W154 was capable of speeds in excess of 190mph.

In the highly skilled and fearless hands of Rudolph Carraciola and Herman Lang it inevitably dominated the 1938 and 1939 Grand Prix seasons. Only a lack of sufficiently high-quality fuel, so the story goes, meant that after the war the W154 had to be put out to pasture.

4 November 1939

The Packard Motor Car Company reveals the first the first ever in-car air-conditioning system. Costing a mere $274.00, the system had no thermostat to control the temperature and took up the entire boot of the car.

1938 **BMW 328**

Germany's early motor-racing history is littered with endless Mercs and Auto Unions, regular evolutions of tried-and-tested ideas, familiar shapes and identical liveries. But one of the true greats of the era was an unlikely upstart from an aircraft engine manufacturer called BMW.

The 328 was a genuine sports car, both in terms of performance and handling, but it managed to bring comfort and refinement to a class more commonly given over to hellish compromise in the hunt for the chequered flag.

The 328 was refined, well appointed and superbly smooth to drive, partly due to its highly sophisticated straight-six (the engine layout BMW swore by for the rest of the century) and partly thanks to advanced and intelligent suspension.

A coupé version of the 328 won the Mille Miglia outright in 1940, setting a record average speed of 103mph. Such extraordinary competition success was made possible because the 328 was immensely light. It featured a radical tubular spaceframe chassis and aluminium and magnesium components, space-aged stuff in the mid-30s. Regrettably, only 461 328s were ever made, with production inevitably nipped in the bud by the start of the war, ensuring that the few cars still in existence command mega-bucks if they ever pop up at auction.

1940 **Volkswagen Kubelwagen** ▶

In the run-up to war, Adolf Hitler recruited no less a chap than Ferdinand Porsche to help him expedite world domination. Quickly devising a lighter, stronger off-road version of his Beetle, he presented the Fuhrer with the nattily named Kubelsitzwagen, or bucket-seat car,

In order to save valuable time the German army shortened the name to Kubelwagen, and soon set about testing it by invading Poland. That went quite well despite a lack of four-wheel drive, thanks to an incredibly low weight and superb off-road agility. By 1940 full production had started and over 50,000 were built before the Allies rolled in and pulled the plug.

1941 **Willys Jeep** ▼

With a beady eye on what Hitler and Porsche were up to in Europe, the Americans began the hurried task of building a rival to the Kubelwagen. After an almighty kerfuffle, the amalgam of three different designs grew into the Willys MB, soon referred to (and no-one's really sure why) as the Jeep.

With its gutsy engine, simplistic, adaptable body and four-wheel drive, the Jeep was ideal military fair and well over 600,000 were produced within the war years. This was also, for better or worse, the grandfather of the modern SUV.

The story of the Tucker '48 saloon is one tainted by injustice. Catching the large US automakers napping, Preston Tucker's '48 brought all sorts of radical and ingenious invention to the industry, with safety an unusual paramount. The '48 had a roll bar, seat belts and even a padded dashboard, alongside a plethora of other impact innovations. It also featured independent suspension, a rear engine configuration and a third, central headlight that turned in the direction you were steering,

From humble beginnings it was, in a word, brilliant. Tragically, one of Tucker's fundraising initiatives was suddenly and ruthlessly investigated by the US government and despite full exoneration later, all the negative publicity brought about at a critical juncture was enough to suffocate the fledgling outfit.

1947 **Cisitalia 202** ▼

Despite a tiny four-cylinder engine borrowed from Fiat, the Cisitalia 202 remains one of the most desirable sports cars of the early post-war years. Hand-built in small numbers, its beautiful lines would come to define a golden age of elegant, understated yet aerodynamic European coachwork. So much so that the Museum of Modern Art in New York has one in its permanent collection.

16 July 1940

Hitler outlines his plans for the invasion of England as the German military machine sits poised on the French coast with some impressive horsepower – real horse power. Around 80% of German transportation is horse-drawn and during the course of the Second World War they will use 2.75 million horses and mules.

1948 **Bristol 401** ▼

With profits plummeting after the Second World War, the Bristol Aeroplane Co. turned its expertise to cars. Using the excellent 2.0-litre straight-six engine from BMW's 328 and 'Superleggera' aluminium bodywork provided by Italian coachworkers Touring, the 401 had the hallmark of greatness.

Performance wasn't up to much, however, with this generously appointed 2+2 failing even to trouble the ton, but outright speed played second fiddle to a peerless overall package. This was refined, impeccably finished stuff for a small and discerning British elite.

12 November 1946

The American love of cars gathers pace as the world's first drive-through bank opens in Chicago.

1948 Unimog ▼

After the war, when Germany was strictly forbidden from building anything with a military bent, it somehow managed to slip the Unimog under the Allied radar. This was, and still is, the mother and father of off-road vehicles, with a hugely powerful Mercedes-Benz diesel engine, gigantic ground clearance and permanent four-wheel drive.

Needless to say, despite its origins as an, ahem, agricultural vehicle, it quickly found favour with the burgeoning West German army and is still in production today, tackling all manner of terrifying environments from desert warfare to jungle fires. This is the Bugatti Veyron of SUVs. Top speed 50mph.

1948 Morris Minor Convertible ▶

The Morris Minor was Britain's answer to the Volkswagen Beetle, but mercifully this similarly affordable, pretty and pretty basic thread in the fabric of our motoring history escaped the cultural sodomy that saw the Beetle turned into a symbol of studenty psychedelia and then reborn as a cynical marketing tool for tragic baby boomers.

The Morris Minor, particularly in convertible 'Tourer' form, is a class act that offered up the open road to the average post-war family and nowadays opens a pleasing little window onto a simpler time, when cheap cars didn't have to be rubbish.

1948 **Jaguar XK120** ▼

The late 40s and early 50s were a bit of a golden age for British motoring, both on road and racetrack. Spearheading this illustrious period was Jaguar, whose comparatively affordable XK120 was unveiled in 1948 and quickly proved to be the fastest production car in the world. The earliest cars were built from lightweight aluminium over an ash frame, although as production increased Jaguar turned to cheaper, more robust steel panels. The extra pounds were ably offset, however, by Jag's superb 3.4-litre straight-six, an engine that acquitted itself commendably at Le Mans and the Mille Miglia in 1950.

1949 **Ferrari 166 MM Barchetta** ▶

Until 1949 Ferrari had focussed its expert energies on racing, so the 166 Barchetta has the grand historic position of being the marque's first purpose-built road-going sports car. This meant stonking performance from its complex 2.0-litre V12 alongside luxury appointments like a hand-stitched leather interior. The combination was inevitably effective, with the 166 taking back-to-back victories at the Mille Miglia in 1949 and 1950 and laying formidable foundations for Ferrari's future.

With the demand for fighter planes on the wane in a newly peaceful Europe, Svenska Aeroplan Aktiebolaget turned its manufacturing skills to a more useful metier. The 92 was Saab's first production car and carried with it the aerodynamic hallmarks of a background in aviation: its drag coefficient, the measure of a car's resistance to air, was on a par with modern-day supercars, And that remarkably slippery single-piece steel body made the best of a weedy two-stroke, two-cylinder engine, with the 92 soon racking up rally wins at home and abroad.

1949 **Rover P4** ▼

The original Rover 75, only referred to as the P4 in later life, was a dramatic and daring slice of affordable luxury when it first appeared in 1949. Borrowing bold styling cues from America, and using an aluminium/magnesium alloy in much of the bodywork, this was a radical rethink from the ancient-looking and overpriced P3. But all was not roses. A conservative British public reacted badly to the third, centrally mounted 'Cyclops' headlight and Rover was forced to remove it. In doing so, however, it sorted out the car's persistent cooling problems, so everyone was happy.

1950s COLD WAR KICKS

While our cousins across the pond apparently did nothing but drink malt shakes and trundle gargantuan, be-chromed V8 drop-tops to drive-in movie lots, the 1950s was a period of some austerity in the UK. Still feeling the pinch after the war, rationing remained, fuel prices were high, steel in short supply and stiff-collared Britishness still prevailed.

As the Cold War rooted itself along Europe's eastern perimeter, families tuned in to the first domestic tellies, only to watch the Russians launching spy satellites and Americans letting off nuclear weapons when they were meant to be at the drive-in. This was a period of paranoid progress, as politics and technology ran amok, little of it for the benefit of the average man in the street.

To make matters worse, it took until 1958 for Britain to come up with an answer to Elvis. And it was Cliff Richard. Things were indeed grim.

But on reflection, from the favourable perspective of the car enthusiast, the 50s was a positive tipping point. It introduced the forbears of such icons as the Porsche 911 and AC Cobra, and saw British motor sport dominate on the world stage. This was a time when it was entirely sensible to drink drive, and smoking was actually good for you. There were no traffic jams and no speed limits, so with the wind in your hair and a cigarette clamped between your wine-stained teeth you could weave your way back from lunch to the office and park right outside without a traffic warden in sight. In fact, what on earth were they complaining about?

1950 **Aston Martin DB2** ▾

One of the definitive sportscar profiles of the 1950s, the Aston Martin DB2 was the first car to carry the monogram of new owner David Brown. This was a man with a clear and determined vision, which extended to buying Lagonda simply so he could take its excellent 2.6-litre straight-six and bolt it to the DB2's tubular chassis.

This was a gigantic step forward from the fusty Aston of old. Modern, elegant, agile and rapid, the DB2 set the standard for future Aston products and raised the bar for all road-going sports cars of its day. A one-two class win at Le Mans that same year threw down the competition gauntlet, too. Aston was back in business...

1950 **Lancia Aurelia GT** ▶

Although markedly less dainty than you might expect from an early 50s Italian coupé, the Aurelia GT remains one the finest grand tourers of its era. Featuring various design firsts for the brand, like a V6 engine and, on later models, high-tech de Dion rear suspension, this was a car that combined impressive performance and luxury – all for a reasonable price. Less than a year after its debut, a near-standard 2.0-litre model placed second in 1951 Mille Miglia, just behind a 4.1-litre Ferrari America. And to underline its point, that same year the Aurelia came first in class at Le Mans.

1950 **Volkswagen Westfalia Camper** ▼

Based on the early Type 2 Transporter, Volkswagen's original split-screen camper was fitted out under license by fellow German company Westfalia. Ingeniously designed, superbly finished, and bolstered by the simplicity and robustness of Volkswagen's air-cooled flat-four, this was the vehicle to open up post-war Europe to the average West German family. However, the Camper was soon to be adopted by America's West Coast hippy culture, badly hand-painted with psychedelic flowers and filled with massive beards and joss sticks.

13 May 1950

A former RAF base welcomes some flying Italians when Giuseppe Farina, Luigi Fagioli and Reg Parnell (okay, he was British) take their Alfa Romeo 158s to first, second and third places in the first Grand Prix of the inaugural Formula 1 championship at Silverstone.

1951 **Jaguar C-Type** ▼

Although overshadowed in the Jaguar pantheon by the D-Type that appeared just three years later, the C-Type was still a formidable competition car in its own right and arguably far easier on the eye. Based on the road-going XK120 Roadster, already acclaimed as the fastest production car in the world some three years earlier, the all-aluminium bodied C-Type was staggeringly fast and focussed, winning the Le Mans 24 Hours at its first attempt.

In 1953 it won again in the hands of Duncan Hamilton and Tony Rolt, this time becoming the first car in the race's history to average over 100mph. Hamilton later revealed that he and Rolt had not expected to race and were up drinking for the entire previous night. Cleared to compete at 10am, their emergency pre-race remedy was coffee, hot baths and double brandies.

1951 **AC Ace** ▼

The AC Ace is hailed by a sizeable portion of motoring's silver-haired cognoscenti as the epitome of British sports car design. The hand-turned aluminium body has a timeless beauty in its elegance and simplicity; the tubular chassis a strength and lightness that translated into remarkably linear and capable handling for the early 50s.

So good to drive was the Ace, in fact, that AC soon started shopping around for more grunt to do its remarkable chassis justice. From its own sweet but modest 100bhp, 2.0-litre, straight-six, AC turned first to Bristol's more modern 120bhp six, then a heavily revised 2.6-litre Ford unit making 170bhp. Then a man called Caroll came a-calling with an idea involving massive American V8s and suddenly the Cobra was born. The Ace was eclipsed for years by its bigger, bulkier brother, but the original car, more lithe, pretty and understated, is suddenly enjoying a renaissance. Auction prices are rocketing and, unlike the Cobra, your neighbour doesn't have a shed-built plastic replica.

1951 **Lamborghini 22PS** ▶

Sometimes we have to raise our glasses in the unlikeliest of directions when endeavouring to catalogue motoring cool, and nowhere more so than here. The Lamborghini 22PS was a rudimentary tractor built from bits of military machinery left over from the Second World War – which obviously begs the question, were the machines in question German or Italian? Probably the former, for Ferruccio Lamborghini made himself a very rich man selling his tractors. Rich enough to buy a Ferrari and be sufficiently unimpressed as to try and build something better. That's how legend has it at any rate. From small acorns, mighty V12 oaks...

1952 **Bentley R-Type Continental** ▼

The R-Type was the sort of car you rode in the back of. If you owned a few newspapers and kept your wives in ermine. The Continental, on the other hand, was very much a car for the driver, albeit the rather British point-and-squirt variety, where gargantuan quantities of power and walnut went before lightness and handling prowess.

The Continental was, in the fashion of Bentley and Rolls-Royce at that time, a chassis and engine with outsourced coachwork, mostly from Mulliner. Built as fastback coupés, the first Conti epitomises mid-50s motoring, with vastness of scale offset by a svelte profile and a withering turn of speed.

29 February 1952

A milestone in the battle between motorists and pedestrians: the first 'Don't Walk' pedestrian-crossing lights are installed in New York City.

1952 **Fiat 8v Zagato** ▼

This must surely be Fiat's zenith, and some 60 years ago at that. The 8v was a small, two-seat coupé born from the company's shelved plans for a mass-production V8 engine. The 8v was sent racing instead, and its bodywork styled by various Italian coachbuilders, Ghia and Pininfarina among them. But the most prolific and successful of these was Zagato, in unusually restrained form it must be said, who produced around 30 8v coupés in both aluminium and steel.

Although not steeped in racing success, there was, and still is, something universally appealing about the compact, subtle and perfectly balanced appearance of the 8v.

◄ 1952 **Morris Minor Traveller**

What makes the Traveller so special, over and above the Minor saloon on which it is based, is that unlikely wooden frame. This was the last British production car to carry on the strange but strangely alluring 'Woodie' tradition that was spawned across the pond in the 1930s.

It was simple, long-lasting and, quite by accident, really rather beautiful.

1953 **Chevrolet Corvette** ▶

The Corvette enjoys a very distinguished position in the Hall of Fast Car Fame. This is, for better or worse – very often worse – the longest-running performance model in history. Older than the Porsche 911. (Almost as old, in fact, as the mass-production, zero performance Volkswagen Beetle.)

It ought to be stressed, however, that while there has never been a truly bad 911, there has seldom been a Corvette that qualified as even half-way good. The C1 that appeared in 1953 features here because it was first. It took until 1960 before a restyled rear made it genuinely pretty. And even then it didn't handle and had a thirst like Richard Burton.

1953 **Porsche 550 Spyder** ▼

The first thing anyone will tell you about the 550 Spyder is that this was the car James Dean killed himself in. It's a crappy legacy for what is surely one of the purest, most attractive shapes in motorsport.

Specifically built for racing, where it earned its reputation as 'the giant killer' amongst the larger, more powerful Jaguars and Mercs of the age, the 550 won its class at Le Mans in its first year. It also racked up further victories on the Targa Florio and the mighty Carrera Panamericana where it first caught the eye of certain wealthy Americans.

Dean owned his 550 for a mere 9 days before his death. He had nicknamed it 'Little Bastard'.

1953 **Moretti 750 Gran Sport Coupé** ▼

Nowadays the name Moretti is usually associated with an Italian beer, but in post-war Turin it meant something very different. In 1945 a motorcycle engine builder called Giovanni Moretti began making exclusive, low-volume sports cars. He was fastidious to the last, creating highly individual and supremely well-finished little cars that soon picked up a small, but loyal, global following.

By the early 50s his tiny 650 and 750cc engines were high-revving works of automotive art which, when combined with beautiful hand-built bodywork by the coachbuilders Michelotti, created one of the prettiest and most entertaining GTs you'll ever see. The 750 Gran Sport is considered Moretti's apotheosis: its design and execution perfect in every respect.

1953 **Triumph TR2** ▶

Designed to steal a slice of MG's burgeoning sales success in the States, the Triumph TR2 was the cheapest 100mph+ two-seater in the UK, but its 2.0-litre straight-four was also good for around 34mpg.
An inevitable and instant hit both at home and abroad, over 8500 TR2s were built in less than three years.

1954 **Toyota Land Cruiser** ▼

In the grand tradition of all good SUVs, the Toyota Land Cruiser started life because of war. Oddly in this case, the Korean War, with an improved Jeep being built on commission by Toyota for the United States Army. Toyota liked what it saw and developed the idea itself. This spawned the BJ, which was mercifully renamed the Land Cruiser in 1954 when full production began. The original Land Cruisers were astonishingly well built and can still be found in active service up mountains and in deserts around the world. Rust, however, has claimed any that went where it's wet.

1954 **AC Aceca** ▶

With the Ace selling faster than AC could make them, the firm began to build a fixed-head version alongside its roadster, also offered with its home-grown engine or the more powerful versions from Bristol and Ford. The Aceca was a slightly more practical car for daily use, made the more so by having a very early hatchback to access the sizeable rear load space.

Sadly the Aceca never got the V8 treatment, with AC instead building bespoke tin-topped Cobras to take on Ferrari at Le Mans.

◄ 1954 **Kaiser Darrin**

Despite the name, Kaiser Motors was actually American and the Darrin a sort of Corvette-a-like, two-seat sports car. Like the Corvette, it too was made of fibreglass in a period when such an idea was radical and not inexpensive. The Darrin had a three-stage folding roof and doors that retracted into the front wings. This sort of thing made it pricey, however, and only 435 were ever made before the company folded in the year of its launch.

1954 **Alfa Romeo BAT 7** ▼

The BAT project was a ground-breaking design experiment by Alfa Romeo in conjunction with the Bertone styling house. BAT stood for Berlinetta Aerodinamica Tecnica, and as the name suggests was an advanced study in airflow. Albeit a deliberately lavish and showy one.

BAT 5, 7 and 9 all appeared in the mid-50s as head-turning concept cars that might have come straight from the set of a dodgy sci-fi movie. But the science was real enough, with the BAT cars achieving incredibly low-drag coefficients that influenced various future designs in high-speed stability.

1954 **Porsche 356 Speedster** ▼

Despite its hallowed position in Porsche's past and present, the origins of the Speedster are comparatively humble. Building on his father's air-cooled, rear-engined, rear-drive vision, Ferry Porsche evolved the Volkswagen Beetle into a sportier coupé and cabriolet, the 356. These sold well in the United States, well enough for Max Hoffman, the sole US importer, to encourage Ferry to design a chop-top roadster version to rival the likes of Jaguar's hugely popular XK120. Far from commanding a premium over the standard car, Hoffman suggested the model in question should be significantly cheaper and therefore more accessible for amateur racers.

The US accounted for around a third of Porsche's entire sales so the idea was taken seriously. The Speedster soon appeared with a paired-back interior spec that included just a speedometer and temperature gauge, unforgiving bucket seats and side screens instead of wind-up windows. A very basic fabric roof and low, heavily-raked windscreen could be removed altogether for weekend competition.

The car was an instant success despite its lack of creature comforts, and has since comprehensively eclipsed the rest of the 356 range for desirability, with high-performance Carrera versions commanding mega-bucks at auction. It's strange to think that one of the most instantly recognised and sought-after cars ever made was in part a cost-cutting exercise. All the more odd that it shares its roots with the VW Beetle.

1954 **Mercedes-Benz 300SL** ▼

1954 was something of a vintage year for the Germans, with Porsche's principal rival also producing one of history's most familiar and desirable shapes. The 300SL, later referred to as the Gullwing because of its vertically hinged doors, was a luxurious road-going revision of Merc's current crop of Silver Arrow racing cars. Coincidentally, the idea to make a street-legal car using the available competition components is also attributed to US importer Max Hoffman. And again he was proved to know his market, with around 80 per cent of all the Gullwings ever made being sold to the US.

With its innovative use of direct-injection, tubular spaceframe chassis and weight-saving aluminium panels, the 300SL became the fastest production car in the world.

It's a curious footnote that those doors, which remain one of the most iconic design features of 20th-century motoring, were the only solution to an awkwardly high sill in the SL's chassis. Even then, Mercedes-Benz had to design a flip-up steering wheel to make access to the cabin possible, and then you could barely reach the doors to close them.

23 November 1954

A 1955 Chevrolet Bel Air two-door coupé rolls off the production line in Flint, Michigan with a very special livery – it is gold plated. The Chevy is the 50-millionth car to be produced by General Motors and, in fact, the bodywork is simply painted gold, although its hundreds of trim parts are regally gold-plated rather than being finished in common chrome.

1954 Jaguar D-Type

There are few cars more synonymous with Blighty's former motoring glories than the Jaguar D-Type, a mid-50s racing car that dominated the Le Mans 24 Hours and proved that form and function really can make happy bedfellows in the right hands.

Combining both extraordinary styling and ground-breaking technology, the D-Type was a formidable milestone in terms of both engineering and racing, with various elements of its radical invention evident on humdrum road cars to this day.

For the less technically minded, the D-Type was little more than a large, racing green phallus with a massive great fin stuck on the back. Which is why they all loved it. For those more inclined towards its engineering minutiae, the D-Type introduced radical and hugely significant advances such as deformable bladder fuel tanks – an idea borrowed from the aviation industry – that made it supremely stable at high speeds and agile in the corners. The D-Type is also credited with being one of the first cars to use a dry sump and disc brakes, and to benefit from aircraft-style aerodynamics, all of which the modern sports car driver takes largely for granted.

It's a cruel irony that the D-Type enjoyed comparatively little success as an official Jaguar product. Teething problems hampered its first outing at Le Mans and a monstrous accident marred its second. But in the privateer hands of Edinburgh-based Ecurie Ecosse, various blue liveried D-Types racked up numerous high-profile wins, including Le Mans victories in '56 and '57.

It remains Jaguar's greatest creation, however, and nearly 60 years since its inception, the D-Type's speed and handling remain pretty astonishing. Truly a car of the future back in 1954, and still not a car of the past today.

1955 **Mercedes-Benz 300 SLR** ▼

There are few cars more intimately entwined in the folklore of motorsport than the Mercedes-Benz 300 SLR. Despite the name, it bore little in common with the 300SL, instead being a pure racer evolved from one of Merc's contemporary Formula 1 cars.

Driven to a legendary victory on the 1955 Mille Miglia by Stirling Moss and his journalist co-driver Denis 'Jenks' Jenkinson, the SLR averaged just under 100mph over that thousand miles of twisting, mountainous public roads.

However, tragedy struck at Le Mans that year in a way that has never been surpassed in motor racing. One of the works SLRs became involved in an unavoidable high-speed collision and somersaulted into the crowd. The driver, Pierre Levegh, died, along with at least 82 spectators.

Despite winning the 1955 World Sportscar Championship, Mercedes-Benz took the decision officially to withdraw from motorsport, a position it would maintain for another 30 years.

1955 **Ford Thunderbird** ▶

Away from the engineering precision and technical wizardry of high-stakes European sports-car racing, the Americans were doing things their own way. As a non-sporting rival to the already not-very-sporty Chevrolet Corvette, Ford launched the Thunderbird in 1955. Realising they had no hope of selling this heavy, underpowered two-seater as a proper sports car, a man called Jonah Lucas Bender came up with a new niche for Ford to stick it in: the personal luxury car.

And although we may chuckle, it worked. The Thunderbird tapped perfectly into the American car-buyer's psyche and comprehensively outsold the Corvette. Here was a small drop-top with all the luxury appointments of a high-end sedan. A legend, albeit a slightly dodgy one, was born.

◀ 1955 **Alpine A106**

This little French coupé was based on very humble Renault running gear beneath a simple fibreglass body. Designed and campaigned by Jean Rédélé, the A106 was to be the first of various highly successful road/rally cars that Alpine produced into the 1970s. They all featured the same essential concept of a Renault engine hung over the rear axle beneath a light and slippery composite body. The A106 managed just 38bhp from its 747cc unit, but this was enough to reach over 95mph.

1955 **Citroën DS** ▶

The DS is regarded as one of the pinnacles of 20th-century design – so much so that the philosopher Roland Barthes wrote an entire essay on it. This was a pioneering product that debuted ideas so advanced and radical that many of them are still fairly cutting-edge today.

There was a semi-auto clutchless gearbox for starters, and a high-pressure hydraulic system for the brakes and transmission. This was the first of many Citroëns to have self-levelling suspension and it trialed new plastics, both on the inside and in parts of the bodywork. So advanced was it that Citroën carried on making it for 20 years.

1955 **Cadillac Eldorado** ▶

There's something about the unashamedly ridiculous Cadillac Eldorado that perfecty encapsulates North America's 'auto industry' in the 1950s. Having debuted two years earlier as a low-volume special build, the Eldorado as we know it appeared in 1955, complete with retina-roasting quantities of highly polished chrome and pointless tail fins.

Dreadful auto-boxes were mated to massively thirsty 6.0-litre V8s that still couldn't make these cars particularly fast, even in a straight line. But somehow none of this mattered. Much like the Ford Thunderbird, this was a luxury lifestyle statement that celebrated a boom time in the US. Fuel was cheap, the roads were empty and the sun was always shining.

1955 **BMW Isetta** ▶

It's incredible to think that the Cadillac Eldorado and BMW Isetta were built in the same century, let alone the same year. You could not hope to find two cars more diametrically opposed, both in terms of physical appearance and design ideology.

Although Italian in origin, it was BMW who made the most of the Isetta's extraordinary bubble-car blueprint. They added a reliable one-cylinder 247cc motorbike engine that could hustle the world's first mass-production micro car to a respectable 53mph. Inside there was plenty of space for two adults and some clobber behind a bizarre hinged nose that acted as the sole means of entry.

Here was a product light years ahead of its time. At a little over seven feet long and weighing less than 350kg, it offered ultra-compact, frugal and dependable urban transport a full half century before such ideas became the car designer's Holy Grail.

1955 **Volkswagen Karmann Ghia** ▼

Volkswagen's workaday Beetle spawned myriad variants, most of them even less desirable. The indisputable exception to the rule, however, was the Karmann Ghia. Although built on a Beetle chassis and using its pedestrian air-cooled engine and humble running gear, its lump-in-throat bodywork was styled by the Italian outfit Ghia, and built by the Germans at Karmann. Too few cars in history have exploited this logical union of artistic ingenuity and manufacturing excellence. The results speak for themselves.

11 June 1955

Tragedy strikes Le Mans as a collision between two cars spills into the assembled crowd, causing the deaths of at least 83 people in the single biggest loss of life in motorsport history.

1955 **Rolls-Royce Silver Cloud** ▶

Where the 1950s commonly marked the start of a more modern approach to design and manufacture, Rolls-Royce was determined to keep it old school. Unitised bodies were becoming the industry norm, but Rolls retained its massive, rigid chassis onto which hefty steel bodywork was bolted.

This body was the single major concession to changing times, however, in that it was assembled by Rolls-Royce rather than being outsourced to bespoke coachworks as was the pre-war norm. How unbecoming was austerity.

Further glimmers of that vulgar modern future were evident on the options lists, with air conditioning available alongside power steering, which proved quite popular on a car that weighed two tonnes.

1955 **Saab Sonett** ▲

In the days before Saab was solely focussed on selling indifferent saloons to advertising executives and dentists, there was the stunning and rapid Sonett. The first of these was purpose-built for racing by a skunkworks team of Saab engineers, with a tiny two-cylinder engine and lightweight GRP bodywork. It is thought as few as six Sonetts were made before rule changes led to Saab pulling the plug on the project. The Sonett would be revived, but never again as a thoroughbred racer, nor in such a beautifully simple guise.

1955 **MGA** ▼

This was the moment when MG hauled itself into the modern age with a total rethink of its increasingly unpopular Morgan-alike TF. The MGA was originally conceived as a racing car, with its curvaceous bodywork and low-slung seating position a massive departure for the brand.

Sold as both roadster and coupé, with a higher performance twin-cam also briefly supplied for amateur competition, the MGA launched the firm as a true global player in the sports car market. Over 100,000 were built with around 90 per cent destined for export, making them tragically rare in the UK today.

◄ 1955 **Messerschmitt KR200**

Like all German manufacturers in the post-war West, Messerschmitt was banned from making anything that could conceivably be construed as having a military application. Playing it exceedingly safe, therefore, but seemingly with a goading edge, it produced the KR200, essentially a fighter plane without any guns, propellers or wings.

With less than 10 horsepower to play with, the KR200 wasn't quick, but it was lively, practical and so much fun that a cabriolet and even a sports-oriented roadster soon followed.

BMW cemented its reputation in the early 1980s as the definitive driver's car, even if the drive in question was no more than a commute. But there were a couple of early exceptions to the suit-and-briefcase design direction, the unlikeliest of which was the 507. Pre-empting the strangely similar 1957 Ferrari 250 GT California, the shark-nosed 507 was also made with the lucrative American market in mind. To that end it was a luxuriously appointed but fast and dynamically superb roadster with optional touring hardtop. Unfortunately for BMW it was also ruinously expensive to build and the resulting ticket price resulted in a sales catastrophe that quickly put the 507, and very nearly BMW itself, to the sword.

30 August 1956

Just six months after the country's first double yellow lines were painted on a road in Slough, it is announced that the first Traffic Wardens are to hit the streets of Britain.

1956 **Aston Martin DBR-1** ▶

The DBR-1 was the first Aston to benefit from homologation changes that allowed cars competing in the World Sportscar Championship to dispense with the need for a road-going equivalent. This gave Aston's designers carte blanche to create an out-and-out racer. Its incredibly low, strong, spaceframe chassis and lightweight body, shifted by a 2.5-litre straight-six, were a combination that put the wind up the establishment at Ferrari and Porsche.

In the string-backed hands of luminaries like Stirling Moss, Jim Clark and Roy Salvadori the DBR-1 became a dominant force in motorsport, taking Aston's first Le Mans victory and the overall championship in 1959.

◀ 1956 **Lotus Eleven**

Lotus boss Colin Chapman was a near religious figure to a generation of motorsport enthusiasts, and the gospel according to Colin was low weight before power. If you could make a car sufficiently light it would be quicker through the corners, ultimately what makes the difference on a racetrack far more often than simple top speed.

Nowhere was this more ably demonstrated than with the Eleven, a purpose-built racer that, full tank of fuel et al, weighed no more than 450kg.

Most commonly fitted with a small but revvy 1100cc Coventry Climax engine, the Eleven racked up numerous class wins at Le Mans, becoming the firm's most successful car after just two years of production.

1956 **Volvo 121/Amazon Coupé** ▶

Although also sold as saloon and estate, it was Volvo's 2-door Amazon that was a runaway success, and this despite some distinctly un-coupé-like proportions.

The tall and bulky two-door Amazon, or 121 as it was known in export markets, was fractionally lighter than the saloon that preceded it and was therefore quickly adopted in its native Sweden as a sports model. This prompted Volvo to equip it with increasingly large and powerful engines, ensuring that a humble, safety-centric family car became something of a race and rally icon.

1957 **DKW 1000 SP** ▶

Part of the Auto Union mothership that eventually became Audi, DKW was known for making small and fairly sensible family cars. The 1000 SP was something of a departure for Dampf-Kraft-Wagen then, in that it was consciously styled as a mini-Ford Thunderbird. But thirsty V8 power was overlooked in favour of a typically modest three-cylinder two-stroke. Sold in limited numbers as both coupé and convertible, the 1000 SP was an improbable but ambitious product of a fledgling West German auto industry.

1957 **Chevrolet Bel Air** ▼

In production for 25 years, the Bel Air was not just a flagship for Chevrolet, but for American culture as a whole. This was the era of white wall tyres and acres of chrome, inside and out. In 1954 revised styling incorporated the familiar tail fins that, by the end of the decade, had grown large enough for short-haul domestic flight.

Sold as both fixed-head and drop-top, the Bel Air was a vast and extravagant lifestyle statement, often finished in head-turning two-tone paint jobs and always powered by a vast, thirsty V8.

1957 **Lancia Flaminia** ▶

The late 50s was another purple patch for Lancia, and some would say its last. The hugely successful and much admired Aurelia was replaced by a more modern but equally attractive coupé in the Flaminia. Styled by Pininfarina and using an evolution of the Aurelia's proven V6, this was an expensive yet subtle 2+2.

But it was the input of coachbuilders Touring that put the Flaminia firmly on the map. They created a shorter, two-seat GT and Convertible with beautiful aluminium bodywork and distinctive twin headlamps. A Sport version also appeared, this time styled by Zagato, and is said to have been described by Enzo Ferrari as one of the best handling cars ever built.

1957 **Porsche 718 RSK Spyder** ▼

An update of the hugely successful 550A, Porsche's 718 RSK improved on aerodynamics and suspension but kept the small, yet technically advanced, normally-aspirated, 1.5-litre quad cam engine. Generating around 140bhp and weighing only 570kg, the RSK was immensely competitive from the outset. It won its class at Le Mans at the second attempt and was outright winner at the Targo Florio in 1959. Unusually, the very narrow and normally left-hand drive RSK could be simply converted to a central driving position, thereby making it eligible for Formula 2 racing as well.

Incredibly few of these cars were made and the strictly competitive nature of its purpose means that fewer still survive.

1957 **Fiat 500**

When your average classic car enthusiast thinks about Italy his, or her, mind will, likely as not, flood with the images, sounds and even smells inextricably linked to high-performance, high-value exotica from Lamborghini, Alfa or Ferrari. But one of the true greats of the Italian stable and a popular contender for most important car of the 20th century is a mass-production model within reach of almost anyone: the Fiat 500.

There are various things that made the 500 special. A tiny, two-cylinder air-cooled rear engine enabled its miniscule, three-metre length to still seat four adults, two of them in something approaching comfort.

That engine configuration and the attendant rear-wheel drive also meant that it was surprisingly good fun to drive and enjoyed some unlikely competition success in the hands of Fiat's Abarth racing division.

But perhaps the thing that made the 500 truly great, and still does to this day, is its ability to overcome all the barriers of gender, wealth and class. Here is a car that appeals to everybody, yet that nobody would resent you for owning. It's a car that makes anyone, man or woman, automatically more attractive to the opposite sex for its loveable styling, self-evident practicality and utter lack of pretension. The 500 is cool because it isn't, and never was, trying to be.

1957 **Maserati 3500 GT** ▼

With a bit of a boom energising the auto industry around the world and demand for ever more exotic and expensive European fare growing exponentially in the States, Maserati went after the volume market with this, the 3500 GT. The marque's first proper grand tourer, the 3500 was a large but graceful 2+2 using an all-new, 3.5-litre straight-six, the first engine Maserati had made that wasn't designed for racing.

The beautiful bodywork was styled by Touring, who had been commissioned to come up with something practical and comfortable for daily use that was still light and sleek enough to remain true to Maserati's hard-fought performance heritage. Although Maserati had started building road cars some 10 years earlier, this is the milestone car that the firm credits with ushering it properly from pit lane to showroom.

16 May 1957

A pink, 1955 Series 60 Cadillac Fleetwood pulls up outside a mansion in the Whitehaven district of Memphis as Elvis Presley moves in to Graceland.

1957 **Lotus Seven** ▼

Legend has it that Colin Chapman sketched out the design of the Lotus Seven on a napkin. And it's a story that only seems more plausible when you actually get near one, or its modern day Caterham equivalent.

There was nothing else half as basic as this on the road, but that's precisely where the Seven's success lay. Available as a home-build kit, it was firstly affordable, secondly easy to put together and thirdly, most importantly, unbelievably good to drive, thanks to low weight and Chapman's superb tubular chassis.

Hair raising at any speed yet capable of out-accelerating sports cars five times its price, the Seven offered an untouchable ratio of bangs for bucks.

1958 **Hindustan Ambassador** ▼

There are few cars as classless as the Hindustan Ambassador. Starting out life in Cowley as the Morris Oxford, the tooling for this solid, basic, steel-bodied saloon was shipped to India in 1958, where Hindustan has kept it in continuous production ever since. The car's simplicity of design and ease of maintenance made it ideal for the demanding conditions of the subcontinent, where it soon touched every walk of life, whether daubed in the familiar black and yellow of the ubiquitous taxi or liveried for the officialdom of police chiefs and government bigwigs. By modern standards it is a truly terrible car, but it's also the ultimate leveller in a country with even more social hang-ups than ours.

◀ 1958 **Alvis TD21 Drophead**

Alvis is one of those little-known British manufacturers, elbowed from centre stage by larger and more prolific rivals like Aston Martin and Jaguar. But the Coventry-based firm was in business for the best part of half a century, and in that time turned out some refined and rather attractive sports tourers.

The TD21 Drophead Coupé was a high point, with a powerful straight-six propelling its not inconsiderable bulk to well over 100mph. It wasn't enormously high-tech by the standards of the day, but it was properly knocked together: Alvis' own limitations meant it outsourced the TD21's bodywork to Park Ward, one of the coachbuilders for Rolls-Royce.

1958 **Austin-Healey Sprite** ▶

Intended from the outset to be an affordable second car for chaps to tinker with on a Sunday morning, the Austin-Healey Sprite was a seriously basic two-seat roadster built by BMC. You got side-screens instead of proper wind-up windows, no external access to the boot space and, only ever mentioned under duress, the engine from a Morris Minor.

But the reality of the Frogeye, as it quickly became known, was rather more rosy. That simplicity enabled industrious and competitive blokes with spanners to turn their Sprites into increasingly competitive club racers.

◀ 1958 **Rover P5**

The P5, actually marketed as the '3-litre' when it debuted in 1958, was a stately saloon and coupé that represented something of a high watermark for the firm. Luxuriously appointed and spacious within, while managing an effective sort of budget grandeur without, the P5 quickly became known as the poor man's Roller.

In a period of unabashed pride in our homegrown industries, Rover was championed throughout society and Queen Elizabeth II is known to have owned and apparently enjoyed driving a P5. But the moment that truly cemented its status as a national institution was in 1979 when Maggie rolled up to take over Number 10 Downing Street in the back of a P5B, a car that was at least six years old.

1958 **Lister Knobbly** ▶

The Knobbly – so called because of its hugely pronounced wheel-arch bulges – was the invention of self-confessed engineering novice Brian Lister. Having raced a bit in the early 50s, he set about building his own car, scavenging parts from various manufacturers and tucking them beneath this distinctive aluminium body.

With no real understanding of aerodynamics, Lister simply endeavoured to make a car with as small a frontal area as possible and keep the weight down further with a tubular spaceframe chassis.

The results were astonishing and the Knobbly unexpectedly competitive. Taking orders from big names in the sport like Caroll Shelby, Lister was soon shipping cars as fast as he could make them. Which, sadly, wasn't very fast as only 17 were ever produced.

◀ 1958 **Lotus Elite**

The Elite, much like anything touched in the Midas fashion of Colin Chapman, broke new ground in sports car engineering. This small, race-bred two-seater was the first in the world to feature a fibreglass monocoque. Although technically Lotus' first production road car, the ultra-light Elite was always built with competition in mind. It went like the clappers for starters, and was also remarkably easy on the fuel, making it an ideal endurance racer. In testament to this, the Elite won its class a staggering six consecutive times at the Le Mans 24 Hours.

1958 **TVR Grantura** ▶

Although not technically the first TVR, the Grantura marked the moment when Trevor Wilkinson's Blackpool-based firm went into something approaching full-blown sports-car production.

Sold as a kit from the off, but also built – infamously badly – by the factory, the Grantura could be had with Ford, MG or Coventry Climax engines. All were modest but the Grantura's proportions and low weight meant that even in the simplest state of tune these were rapid, demanding and highly entertaining little drivers' cars.

The Grantura stayed in production for the best part of a decade, evolving in style and chassis structure to accommodate increasingly large and powerful engines. The finances remained shaky at TVR, as they would for 50 years, but the customers kept coming.

1958 **Citroën 2CV Sahara** ▼

The 2CV is itself something of a legend these days, with its sardine tin construction and white knuckle handling, but the one that warrants a position here is the Sahara. This was an extremely low-volume, off-road version of the basic 2CV that differed in one fairly major way. It had an engine under the bonnet as usual, but then one in the boot for good measure. Complicated to engineer and therefore twice the price of the standard 2CV, the Sahara was a sales disaster. The only significant uptake came from Spain's Guardia Civil and the weather-weary Swiss postal service.

5 December 1958

Harold Macmillan opens the UK's first motorway, a two-lane behemoth that ran for 8.25 miles.

1959 **Austin-Healey 3000** ▶

Built by BMC for almost a decade before Austin-Healey finally turned up its toes, the 3000 was a mighty last hurrah. The first of the 'Big Healeys', the Mk1 3000 used the in line-six from Austin's Westminster saloons but draped it beneath bodywork fabricated by Jensen. It was rapid, comfortable and easy to work on – very British in essence. But the styling, emphasised by the popular two-tone paint-jobs, had echoes of early Corvettes, ensuring cross-pond appeal then and now.

1959 **Austin-Healey Sebring Sprite** ▲

The ultimate evolution of Austin-Healey's loveable budget sports car was the legendary Sebring. So heavily modified were the Sebrings – named to celebrate a 1-2-3 class win in the Florida endurance race for three works Sprites – that they became recognised by motorsport's governing body as a make in their own right. The most famous and desirable Sebrings are the all-aluminium fixed-head GTs that soon became a dominant force in small-capacity series around the world, driven to countless class wins by Stirling Moss, among others.

1959 **Facel Vega HK500** ▼

The HK500 was the final evolution of the first grand tourer offered by small French firm Facel Vega. These were imposing and exceptionally well-made luxury coupés – alongside a handful of slightly wobbly convertibles – that offered immense luxury and exclusivity in a rapid, comfortable and practical 2+2. Facel's advertising hook was 'for the few who own the finest'. The last of the HK500s were fitted with Chrysler's 6.3-litre V8, enabling it to get remarkably close to 150mph. Serious speed in the late fifties, especially for a car of this bulk.

◀ 1959 **Daimler SP250**

The SP250 seems like a blip in the otherwise very grand and hefty line of limousines that were Daimler's speciality. Oddly styled in fibreglass as a be-finned drophead with a small rear bench, the SP250's main selling point was a bespoke 2.5-litre V8.

It was exceedingly quick for the time but suffered from a lack of rigidity in the chassis. So bad was it that the doors were known to pop open under heavy cornering loads, which did little for the car's sporting reputation. When Jaguar bought Daimler it endeavoured to rectify the SP250's problems, but actually only compounded them by launching the E-Type a couple of years later.

1959 **Sunbeam Alpine** ▶

A frustrated footnote in the story of British motoring, Sunbeam was a pre-war colossus that got walloped by the Great Depression. It reappeared in name alone under the Rootes Group, the conglomerate behind the likes of Hillman and Talbot.

The Alpine began life in 1953, but these early cars were clumsily styled and cumbersome to drive. A total revision was embarked upon three years later and in '59 the Series 1 appeared, a desirable and affordable sports tourer. It wasn't particularly fast, but it was pretty to behold and enjoyable to drive. Perhaps not really worthy of the Sunbeam name, but a coup for Brits on a budget.

1959 **Ferrari 250 GT SWB** ▼

The late 50s and early 60s were a tumultuous time at Ferrari, with huge successes born through bitter internal rivalries. The greatest model in the marque's remarkable history, the 250, arrived in the thick of it all, and in 1959 spawned the GT Berlinetta SWB. The SWB, standing for 'short wheelbase' is regarded as the last true dual-purpose Ferrari, in that it was sold in near identical states as both luxury grand tourer and outright racer. The most highly prized and successful of these had aluminium bodywork to make the best of Ferrari's unusually light and powerful 3.0-litre V12. Styled by Pininfarina, built by Scaglietti, raced by Stirling Moss, this is a car surpassed for significance and desirability only by its own evolution, the 250 GTO.

1959 **Ferrari 400 Superamerica** ▶

While Ferrari was building and racing highly technical sports cars it was also in the entirely logical business of making opulent, limited and very expensive tourers to fund its competition exploits.

These cars were known as the America series, pitched squarely at the wealthy US market where large-capacity V12s and dramatic touring bodywork could, and did, command eye-watering prices.

Cash cows though they may have been, the Americas were built on the 250 GT chassis and were every inch as fast and capable as they looked. Pinin Farina's designs, both in coupé and cabriolet form, were not only beautiful but highly aerodynamic. Only 47 were sold in just under five years of production, making every one of this highly individual series exceptionally rare and sought-after today.

1959 **Maserati Tipo 61 (Birdcage)** ▼

The Tipo 61 earned the universal moniker 'Birdcage' due to its extraordinarily complicated tubular spaceframe chassis. A bewildering design of small gauge tubing, intricately woven together, created a very strong but light frame over which Maserati folded impossibly curvaceous low-drag bodywork.

The cars looked stunning and were genuinely competitive, when they worked. Back-to-back wins at the Nürburgring 1000KM were the Tipo 61's racing highpoint, with the Blue Riband of Le Mans eluding them due to reliability problems.

1960s
TURN ON, TUNE IN, DROP CLUTCH

I t's essential to remember that the 60s were not 'swinging' if you were a proper chap. If you liked sports cars, owned them, raced them, any of that, then kaftans, bongs and the clap were other people's problems.

You had a sports jacket and a dark tie and probably some of those suede shoes that made double de-clutching a bit smoother. Even though syncromesh had made your carefully honed skills there all but obsolete.

The 60s were, for the true motoring enthusiast, really just the 50s but with engineering improvements and a speed limit. Cars were still comparatively cheap, as was fuel. Sports car racing was in its heyday with the gentleman amateur still in evidence. This was a magnificent period for Brits, Germans, Italians and even Americans – a decade in which all the great motoring nations excelled at some level, producing fabulous road and race cars that now make up the core of what most of us regard as classics.

Obviously there was a lot else going on. War with Communism in Vietnam, and Israel vs Everyone Else in the Middle East. The Berlin Wall popped up, as did some major left-wing figureheads, who promptly got shot. There was the Cuban Missile Crisis to keep the West on its toes for a few weeks, and even a man on the moon by the end of the decade. Throw in the aforementioned social haymaker of a counter-cultural revolution and you'd think there was a lot more to get excited about than just cars. But you'd be wrong, really, when you remember that civil rights and acid can't hold a candle to an AC Cobra. That a single decade can be responsible for the Cobra, Ferrari 250 GTO, the Porche 911 and the Aston Martin DB4 GT Zagato simply beggars belief. LSD stands for limited slip differential. It always did.

1960 Porsche 356B Carrera ▼

The 'B' variant was Porsche's most numerous 356, and it was with this model that the race-honed Carrera really found its stride. With its engine enlarged to 2.0-litres and now developing 130bhp, the Carrera could see off 60mph in under ten seconds and only ran out of puff at 125mph. This bettered many far more powerful and exotic sports cars and GTs of the period.

Part of the Porsche's secret was that it was significantly lighter than the standard coupé, thanks to a ruthlessly stripped-out interior. But the true genius lay in the high-revving and wildly complicated four-cam engine. To this day, the Carrera's four-cam is the stuff of legend, and repairing it the stuff of nightmares.

12 September 1960

In response to the alarming number of accidents reported on the country's roads, the Ministry of Transport introduced the MOT test for all cars over 10 years old.

1960 **Aston Martin DB4 GT Zagato** ▼

By 1960, Ferrari's dominance of sports car racing was becoming depressing. So two years after the launch of the DB4 GT, Aston Martin dropped in on Italian coachworkers Zagato and one of the great partnerships in motoring history was formed.

The standard DB4 was designed as a gentleman's grand tourer, with comfort taking precedence over outright speed and handling. This meant that it was heavy and soft, and therefore unlikely to trouble the chequered flag.

Zagato set about making the car shorter, lower, vastly lighter and even a bit more powerful. But there wasn't much they could do about the softness, and when their stunning creation finally took to the track it still never really stood a chance.

But of course, no one cares. The DB4 GT Zagato was then and still is one of the most beautiful and individual sporting GTs, made all the more desirable by its immense scarcity. Only 19 original units were ever made and they now change hands for millions of pounds.

1961 **Renault Alpine A110** ▶

From the immensely humble origins of a rebuilt Renault 4CV, by 1961 little French rally expert Alpine had a car that was really mixing it with the international big boys. Although continuously in development, the A110 was always a simple thing, with steel backbone chassis, fibreglass bodywork and a huge amount of its mechanical componentry scavenged from road-going Renaults – which is what makes its achievements all the more remarkable. Increasingly competitive throughout the following decade, by the early 70s the A110 had begun to win at the highest level. And when the first World Rally Championship was held in 1973, it was a factory-run Alpine A110 that took the title, leaving the Porsche and Lancia establishment with no answers.

1961 **Volvo P1800** ▶

It seems impossible for anyone to mention the Volvo P1800 without automatically also mentioning that Roger Moore drove one in camp 60s telly series 'The Saint'. This means little to those not cashing in their pensions, and the superbly styled and impressively robust P1800 deserves a better legacy.

For starters, this was the only car Volvo had ever made that looked in any way cool. And they'd been around for thirty years by this point. Some might say that fact still stands some forty years after the P1800 finished production.

Sold as both 2+2 coupé and immensely stylish yet practical shooting brake, the P1800 was sprightly if not particularly quick and, after the first few years, immensely well built.

◀ 1961 **Ginetta G4**

Ginetta's USP has always lain in getting the average man onto the grid. And nowhere was this more successfully achieved than with the G4, a small, attractive and extremely capable two-seater that was sold as a comparatively affordable kit.

The self-build concept made a lot of sense to the tinkering amateur, who could use his car on the road during the week then take it racing, unaltered, on a Sunday morning.

The G4, powered by highly tuneable Ford engines that made the most of its light tubular spaceframe and GRP body, were incredibly good considering their garden-shed provenance, and earned a deserved reputation as giant slayers on the international sports car circuit.

1961 **Triumph TR4** ▶

Essentially a cosmetic evolution of the hugely successful and popular TR3, the '4' offered modern amenities such as wind-up windows and heater vents in the dash, all enveloped in a more contemporary body by the Italian styling house Michelotti. The TR4 also benefited from an optional hard top with removal panels, creating the 'Targa' top some years before Porsche made it their own.

The car was another sales success for Triumph, who continued to peddle the majority to an eager American market. Here it was taken racing by works teams and privateers to great success, including a class win at Sebring.

1961 **Lagonda Rapide** ▼

With only 55 ever built, retailing at five times the price of the TR4 opposite, the luxurious power of Aston's Lagonda Rapide was a serious indulgence by anyone's standards. Built on a stretched DB4 chassis with elegant four-door bodywork expertly executed by Italian coachworks Touring, the Rapide was then equipped with the powerful, four-litre, twin-cam straight-six that would later appear in the DB5. With various advanced innovations in out- and on-board luxury, like electric windows, servo-assisted disc brakes and heated screens, the Rapide managed to introduce an extra element of practicality and comfort to David Brown's line-up without betraying the firm's essential sporting focus.

22 December 1960
Morris produced a commemorative run of 349 lilac-liveried Minors to mark the millionth Morris Minor to roll off of the production line.

1962 **Ferrari 250 GTO**

This is the car that unites obsessive collectors, oil-rich oligarchs, rock stars and wrinkly racers, commanding ridiculous multiples of millions on the rare occasions one ever makes it to auction. More often than not, however, they are sold in secret for undisclosed sums to be squirreled away in private collections, and for this reason it's impossible to put an accurate value on the fabled Ferrari 250 GTO. Safe to say it has a strong claim to being the most expensive car in history, yet still it is raced in anger on a regular basis. Enzo Ferrari would be tap-dancing in his grave.

The GTO is the apotheosis of Ferrari's 250 line, the ultimate evocation of what many would argue is the ultimate sports car. Built to take part in the FIA's newly revised GT Championship, it was designed by Bizzarrini and bodied by Scaglietti, evolving the 250 GT SWB with far greater attention to aerodynamics and adding yet more power. This came from a highly tuned, 3.0-litre V12, dry-sumped and with six Weber carburettors.

It wasn't a hugely sophisticated set-up by the standards of the day, with its aluminium panels riveted to a steel tubular chassis and a big lump up front, but its combination of lightness, power and stability at speed proved to be a winning one. The GTO took the GT series for three years on the trot, establishing itself as the last, great, front-engined race-car. Fierce battles always ensued, especially at Le Mans, where the Ferrari went toe-to-toe with Ford's V8-powered AC Cobras, creating one of motorsport's most epic rivalries. But the GTO came out on top, and continued to rack up race wins for years to come both in factory and privateer hands.

Incredibly basic inside, with no concessions to comfort and refinement, the 250 GTO is a purist's racer for which competition provenance is key. Fewer than forty were ever made and yet, perhaps unremarkably, all survive in good order today. Start saving.

1962 **Ogle SX1000** ▶

The quintessence of shoestring British engineering, the Ogle SX1000 was a Mini rebodied as a little fibreglass coupé. But making BMC's increasingly ubiquitous city car into something more exclusive and desirable seemed like a stroke of genius, with customers able to supply their own Mini or buy a completely converted Cooper with performance to match its pocket-rocket looks.

Tragically, and rather awkwardly from a PR point of view, David Ogle killed himself in an SX1000, and production stopped after a mere 66 cars had been finished.

1962 **Peel P50** ▶

A few years and a few bob of investment behind BMW's Isetta, Britain came up with its own urban transport solution. Although technically it wasn't Britain, it was the Isle of Man, which might go some way towards explaining the mad genius of the Peel P50.

A tiny single-seater with one door and no reverse gear, the Peel weighed just 59kg, which meant its 49cc engine could find a tidy top speed of 38mph.

The Peel's real claim to fame, however – and it isn't a surprising one – lies in being the smallest production car of all time. More relevant now than ever before, the Peel is back in production under new owners, with a claimed fuel economy of over 200mpg.

16 April 1962

The American muscle car takes a leap forward with the announcement that Oldsmobile is to fit its F-85 Jetfire with turbocharged petrol engines, a first for road cars.

1963 **Chevrolet Corvette Sting Ray** ▶

The second generation Corvette debuted both as traditional convertible and an all-new fixed-head coupé, with futuristic angles, pop-up headlights and a general sense of the space age into which America was charging headlong. But the grand tradition of Corvettes remained, with a fairly agricultural steel chassis and massive V8 enveloped in fibreglass. There were some concessions to modernity, such as disc brakes and wishbone suspension, but in reality this was still simple stuff, which kept the cost down and repairs simple.

The coupé was the real headturner, with its trademark split rear screen a unique and striking design feature. Sadly, concerns about rearwards visibility put paid to that after just one year of production, making those early hard-tops some of the most collectible and valuable Corvettes ever made.

1963 **Hillman Imp** ▼

The Imp is one of those weird cars that, despite being designed with rather humble domestic duties in mind, quickly became a much-modified and unexpectedly sporty little coupé.

Having a de-tuned version of the endlessly re-tuneable Coventry Climax engine tucked into its rear was clearly too much of a temptation, and the Imp enjoyed an unexpected degree of rally and race success, including winning the British Saloon Car Championship three years running.

1963 **Ferrari 250 LM** ▶

Of the bewildering array of model variants that sprang from Ferrari's all-conquering 250 series, one of the most distinctive and unusual is the LM. Using chassis technology from its first mid-engine Formula 1 car, the 250 LM shoehorned the GTO's massive and mighty 3.3-litre V12 behind the driver. First created for the prototype racing class as an open-top competition special, the 250P, the enclosed LM was entered as a GT and therefore had to be sold as a road car, too. Although never quite matching the on-track successes of the prototype, the LM was a milestone for Ferrari as the first road-going, mid-engined V12.

1963 **Gordon Keeble GK-1** ▼

Little known and impossibly rare, the Gordon Keeble GK-1 ought to be the greatest car ever made. A classic British grand tourer, designed by Italian icon Giugiaro for Bertone, and powered by a 5.4-litre Chevy V8 from the Corvette, it had all the elements required to be an unstoppable force in mid-60s motoring. It was fast, light – thanks to fibreglass bodywork – sturdily built and luxuriously equipped, making it every bit a match for contemporary rivals like the ISO Rivolta and Ferrari 330 GT. Unfortunately, this made the Gordon Keeble expensive, which is not a good thing for a car no-one's heard of, and in no time the money ran out. Only 104 cars were ever made, 90 of which can still be accounted for.

1963 **Lamborghini 350 GT** ▼

The tale of Lamborghini's origins – a feud with Enzo Ferrari over a car that the tractor magnate was unhappy with – is the stuff of apocryphal legend. The very real consequence was this, the 350GT.

Lamborghini had a lot of money and set about roping in the best engineers he could lay his hands on. His directive was actually very different from Enzo's, matching performance and handling with refinement and comfort. So a Bizzarrini designed V12 was detuned to be more tractable and reliable. Sleek Scaglione bodywork was softened to make it more spacious inside and practical for luggage. Understated beauty and reliable performance. Ferrari may well have lost some sleep in '63.

◄ 1963 **Maserati Quattroporte**

Although now into its fifth evolution, the first Quattroporte was easily the finest. Rapid, comfortable and blessed with an understated class, this was one of a tiny handful of four-door saloons that could offer performance to rival the sports cars of their time.

1963 **Mercedes-Benz 600 Pullman** ▼

Favoured by despots and Hollywood royalty, the Mercedes-Benz 600 Pullman, also known as the Grosser, was the last word in limousine luxury. Heavier than God's own dumbbells and well over six-metres long, the Pullman was as complicated as it was massive thanks to adventurous engineering experiments like hydraulically powered doors and seats which, back in '63, must have made the it feel like the USS Enterprise. As would the 'waft-along' air suspension – the only solution for a near-three tonne kerbweight.

1963 Trabant 601 ▶

The 'Trabi' was the definitive transport solution for anyone unlucky enough to find themselves on the chillier side of the Iron Curtain. Mass-produced in East Germany for almost 30 years, the Trabant 601 was Communism's answer to the Volkswagen Beetle but somehow vastly cooler then and now. Powered by a crude and unreliable two-stroke engine, the Trabant was a bastard to keep going and fairly lethal in a prang, a reputation worsened by the use of bizarre composite body panels made out of recycled cotton.

◀ 1963 Mercedes-Benz SL

Perhaps one of the prettiest and most enduring automotive outlines there ever was, the 1963 Mercedes-Benz 230SL achieved as much by not really trying terribly hard. This wasn't a performance-focussed sports car, nor was it an extravagant grand tourer, instead it was a sensibly appointed, superbly finished, practical and mildly entertaining 2+2 with the sort of timeless appeal that its modern equivalent can only dream of.

Although sold as a roadster, it was the car's elegant detachable hardtop that kept buyers coming right into the 70s, and earned it the nickname 'Pagoda'.

1963 Ford Lotus-Cortina ▶

With Ford in America creating muscle cars out of stock saloon cars, so the Blue Oval in Blighty felt the need to put a little lead in the Cortina's pencil. But without a parts-sharing, V8-powered big brother model from which to scavenge, Ford were obliged to look closer to home. Enter Colin Chapman and his Lotus chums. They lightened it, seriously improved the suspension and fitted a free-revving twin-cam engine to a close-ratio Lotus gearbox. Driven by the likes of Jim Clark and Jackie Stewart, the Ford Lotus-Cortina utterly dominated British saloon-car racing and claimed countless class wins around the world.

1963 **Maserati Mistral** ▼

This was the final outing for Maserati's lauded twin-cam straight-six, an engine with its roots in Formula 1, before the company began focussing on the world of V8s. The Mistral was sold as both fixed-head coupé and drop-top spyder from 1964 to 1970, for a while alongside its bigger, more American-influenced Ghibli sibling.

Designed by Pietro Frua, who audaciously recreated this exact look for AC a few years later, the Mistral was a compact but comfortable sporting GT. Full of character from that complex, free-revving engine, yet hugely practical thanks to a big glass hatchback, the pretty and rapid Mistral is regarded by some as the last great Maser.

22 November 1963

The X-100, a 1961 Lincoln Continental four-door convertible, is impounded following the assassination of President Kennedy in Dallas. The car in which the president was shot is later refurbished, fitted with a transparent armoured hardtop and ultimately remained in White House service until 1977.

1963 **Jaguar E-Type Lightweight** ▶

The success of the E-Type as a road car has a lot to do with its unlikely performance-to-price ratio, which outstripped anything else on sale, but Jaguar was under no illusions as to the competitive prospects of its soft, comfortable grand tourer.

So, for one year only, the Coventry firm set about making a limited number of highly tuned, lighter and far more uncompromising racing E-Types. Using aluminium panels and componentry, and upping the 3.8-litre straight-six to 300bhp, the Lightweights were far closer to the D-Type from which many of their design initiatives had grown. Only 12 ever left the factory and despite never making a serious impression at the highest level of motorsport, these tractable thoroughbreds are an amateur racer's dream today.

1963 **Aston Martin DB5** ▼

Perhaps the most instantly recognisable car in history, thanks to a certain bed-hopping secret agent, Aston Martin's DB5 was in truth a far cry from this icon of knicker-snapping machismo when it first appeared in 1963. Light controls and an immense sense of high-end civility, bolstered by cutting-edge indulgences like electric windows and optional air conditioning, made this the perfect cosseting grand tourer for the refined and delicate English gent. Or even, dare we say it, his other half. Still rapid, still beautiful, but definitely a tiny bit girly.

1963 **Shelby/AC Cobra**

The story of the AC Cobra is *Boy's Own* stuff, with a small and plucky Anglo-American team of engineers and racers taking on the nefarious might of Enzo Ferrari in his prime. It didn't quite end in a shower of champagne and trophies, but the epic battles fought on an international stage gave birth to one of motoring's most majestic and desirable icons.

Carroll Shelby, the man behind the Cobra, was a successful racing driver in his own right who had won Le Mans in 1959. Having moved into business importing the AC Ace, he quickly recognised the unusual dynamic abilities of the underpowered roadster and approached the firm with a request that they build him a version modified to accept a V8. AC agreed and with Ford's newly designed lightweight V8 on board, a competition legend was clearly in the offing.

Quickly growing from 4.2 to 4.7-litres, the Cobra completely dominated every North American motorsport event it entered. It was also sold in limited numbers as a road car both in the United States and Europe. These were incredibly fast and powerful for the time and, despite their humble origins and lack of historic pedigree, were highly sought after.

The Cobra's journey from domestic to international sporting dominance would be a bumpier one, however, with the comparably powerful and more aerodynamic Ferrari 250 GTO better suited to the high-speed circuits of GT racing. This called for a return to the design studio and, a year later, the ultimate evolution of Shelby's brilliant vision, would appear. The gloves were well and truly off...

1964 **AC Daytona Coupé** ▼

Even when it's not a Ferrari, it seems we have Ferrari to thank: this time for one of the great phallic outlines in motorsport. The AC Daytona Coupé was a Cobra with vastly improved aerodynamics, designed to emulate the ridiculous speeds of the all-conquering 250 GTOs.

Retrospectively nicknamed after the car's debut outing, the Daytona was able to pass 180mph, actually faster than the Ferrari. After winning the GT class at Le Mans at its first attempt, the following year it took the championship. Enzo's nose was seriously out of joint.

1964 **Marcos 1800** ▶

When Jem Marsh and Frank Costin revealed the Marcos 1800, a few eyebrows were raised. Not because of the styling, which was risky but effective, but because the chassis was made of plywood.
Costin's background in aviation had made him something of an expert in lightweight rigidity, however, and the Volvo-powered 1800 proved to be a giant slayer, both on the road and race track.

1964 **Sunbeam Tiger** ▶

Following in the foolproof footsteps of Caroll Shelby, another Anglophile American decided to shoehorn a vast V8 into a delicate British sportscar. The underpowered inpatient was the Sunbeam Alpine. The post-operative product of Ian Garrad's vision – with Shelby's expert team doing the oily bits – was the Tiger.

Although lacking the outright pace of the Cobra, the Tiger was as practical as it was quick, ensuring massive success in the States.

1964 **Meyers Manx** ▶

Yet another car with a Volkswagen Beetle at its heart, the Meyers Manx is one of those universally recognised designs for which the designer is seldom credited.

Bruce Meyers used a chopped-down Beetle chassis and running gear with his simple but inspired 'Beach Buggy' fibreglass body. It was fast, solid and versatile enough to complete the Baja 1000 in record time, sending the Manx global. Hundreds of replicas soon appeared and because of the simplicity of his design, Meyers was deemed powerless to maintain a patent.

1964 **Morgan Plus Four Plus** ▶

Morgan is famous for having changed almost nothing about its cars since the company was founded in 410 BC. But that's not entirely fair. They have tried once or twice, and the first effort was actually quite a fine one. The 'Plus Four Plus' was a Plus Four plus a roof. And the streamlined fibreglass bodywork not only looked great, it was also lighter than the Plus Four minus, making it faster and more nimble.

1964 **Renault 8 Gordini** ▼

Gordini was a tiny little French racing outfit that occasionally sprinkled some motorsport magic on to otherwise rather humdrum Renaults. Its most celebrated act of sorcery is probably the Renault 8 Gordini, a sporting take on an otherwise rather ordinary early-60s saloon. Finished in what would become a trademark French blue with twin white stripes, the 8 Gordini was fitted with a larger 1108 cc engine that delivered its increased power more aggressively via a close-ratio gearbox. Lower, stiffer suspension and disc brakes completed the transition from three-box commuter to semi-competition spec giant killer.

1964 **Mini Cooper S** ▶

Much was made of the Mini's handling prowess at its launch in 1959, to the consternation of BMC's top brass. But by 1964 the stiffs in suits were eating humble pie by the lorry load as a Cooper S romped home to win the Monte Carlo Rally.

The brainchild of John Cooper, race engineer and chum of the Mini's designer, Alec Issigonis, the Cooper S, with its race-tuned 1275cc engine, disc brakes and twin carbs was astonishingly fast and agile. It continued to dominate rally competition for the next three years, firmly rooting the Mini brand in the public consciousness as one of the definitive symbols of plucky British endeavour.

◀ 1964 **NSU Wankel Spider**

The NSU's pretty little Spider was a test bed for a new kind of engine: the Wankel. This was a small-capacity rotary unit that has more recently appeared to greater acclaim in the Mazda RX-8. But back then it was a touch unreliable, making serious production of the Spider impossible.

The few that were made are highly collectible, however. Styled by Bertone, the Wankel Spider was good-looking, free-revving and rapid, with its rear-engine configuration providing unexpectedly sporty handling.

1964 **Mini Moke** ▼

Off to one side, while Mini was cleaning up on the international rally circuit, a rather less glamorous product was making its way to market. Originally intended for military use but evidently unlikely to fit the bill, the frill-free Moke was eventually sold in reasonable numbers on civvy street.

Essentially a boil-washed jeep without the four-wheel drive, the doorless, roofless Moke was hopelessly ill-equipped to deal with the vagaries of its home climate but soon became a hit in the colonies. Mokes can now be found as far afield as Australia and the Caribbean, but are like hen's teeth on soggy home soil.

1964 **De Tomaso Vallengula** ▶

Ultra-rare and virtually still-born, the Vallengula was a De Tomaso road project that never received the sort of financial backing required to turn it into a proper production car. A small, mid-engine two-seater cannibalising parts from Ford and Volkswagen, it was De Tomaso's first road car and shared suspension parts with its own F3 racers.

Handling was superb but, with its engine mounted directly to a steel backbone chassis, it was incredibly raw and unrefined. Only 50-odd were made before De Tomaso turned its attention to the more familiar Mangusta.

1964 **Iso Grifo** ▼

Doubtless owing some of his inspiration to Gordon Keeble, Iso owner Renzo Rivolta sought to mate his native Italian style with American muscle in a luxurious grand tourer. Borrowing the powerful, reliable, 5.4-litre V8 from the Chevrolet Corvette, Rivolta then enlisted former Ferrari engineer Bizzarrini to design a chassis and Giugiaro to design the body. The results were predictably compelling. Beautiful, dynamically capable and fast, the Iso Grifo was as rapid as far-pricier peers while managing to be both more practical and better looking.

1964 **Ford GT40** ▼

The origins of the legendary GT40 are, like so many motoring icons, credited to Ferrari. Ford in the US was a mighty and formidable empire, but Henry Junior wanted international recognition. So he set his sights on Le Mans, and in the early 60s there was only one way to win that: buy out Ferrari.

Enzo played ball for a while but pulled out of lengthy and expensive negotiations at the last minute. Henry was piqued and set about building his own car to humiliate Enzo on a world stage. The GT40, Ford powered and designed by Lola, evolved through a couple of years of indifferent competition to utterly dominate Le Mans in 1966 with a one-two-three finish. With its mid-mounted 7.0-litre V8 and incredibly low bodywork – the '40' refers to the car's height in inches – the GT40 became a distinctive and familiar sight at the chequered flag, winning Le Mans four years straight. Enzo was suitably chastised.

1964 **Pontiac GTO** ▶

Shamelessly nicking the GTO moniker from Ferrari, General Motors offshoot Pontiac slapped it onto a stock V8 road car. A vast and fairly crude coupé and convertible that evolved through a bewildering number of style changes throughout the next decade, it nevertheless became idolised in the States as a symbol of the no-nonsense, blue-collar working man. The Ford Mustang was just around the corner, but it is the GTO that can lay claim to being the world's first muscle car.

1964 **Ford Mustang** ▶

Hot on the heels of the Pontiac GTO, Ford unveiled its own muscle car, the enduring and now legendary Mustang.

Giving rise to the pony car class of two-door, four-seat coupés with a V8 spinning up the rears, the Mustang was a straightforward piece of mid-sixties engineering, using as much available componentry as possible from contemporary Ford models. This made it cheap to build, service and maintain. Which is exactly what Ford bosses, Ford dealers and Ford customers wanted.

Sold as a fixed head with saloon boot, as a convertible and as an elegant but practical fastback, the Mustang was a dizzying success, with Ford struggling to meet the frenzied demand for a car that, although now a shadow of its former self, has stayed in continuous production ever since.

1965 **Bizzarrini Rivolta Daytona** ▶

They don't get any rarer than the Iso Rivolto Daytona. This was a one-off, commissioned by a wealthy Milanese chap called Carlo Bernasconi who kept hold of it for almost thirty years. Essentially a rebodied version of the racing Grifo, it used not only Bizzarinni's excellent chassis but also his outlines for the bodywork. Stunningly beautiful and latterly proven to be very competitive in vintage endurance and hill climbs, the Daytona has the spark of true greatness, dampened only by its own obscurity.

1965 **Lola T-70** ▶

It's not race success that makes the Lola T-70 such a standout from the mid-sixties, for there wasn't much of that, but instead its jaw-dropping aerodynamic outline. Honed in a wind tunnel, it went beyond the contemporary conventions of minimising drag and used its swept-up tail to create downforce, giving it a real advantage in the high speed chicanes and corners like Le Mans' Sarthe. Unfortunately a lack of funding and reliability issues left it outclassed by Ford's GT40 and later the Porsche 917. Always the bridesmaid then, but a looker.

1965 **Rolls-Royce Silver Shadow** ▼

The Silver Shadow is probably the most immediately familiar Rolls-Royce shape. Which is a bit of a shame as it's far from the firm's best, but this is the car that hauled Rolls into the latter half of the 20th Century.

For the first time, the archaic ladder chassis and separate steel body panels were dispensed with in favour of a monocoque, enabling the Silver Shadow to be lighter, stiffer and more spacious within. It also benefited from independent rear suspension with hydraulic self-levelling that created its famously smooth ride quality. This was thoroughly modern stuff for the Roller demographic, enough to keep the company resting on its laurels again for a decade and a half before the next model turned up.

1965 **AC 428** ▼

As if to underline the excellent job Pietro Frua felt he had done on the Maserati Mistral, he did it all over again for the AC 428. This was the successor to the Cobra, but a significant departure with its GT styling and commodious proportions. It was still seriously quick, however, thanks to a 385bhp, 7.0-litre V8 mated to the final Cobra 427's superb, fully independent chassis. But with an American engine, Italian bodywork and that British chassis to bring them together, this was an expensive car to make, a problem that was passed on to the customer. And they voted with their feet. As few as 50 coupés and 30 convertibles were made before AC turned off the lights.

1965 **Alfa Romeo Guilia TZ2** ▶

A far cry from the humble road-going Giulia, the TZ2 was more like a baby Ferrari 250 GTO. In 1961 a former employee of both Alfa and Ferrari, called Carlo Chiti, had set up Autodelta, an independent Alfa racing division. Two years later he created the original TZ using a bespoke tubular spaceframe and lightweight bodywork from Zagato. The TZ, for Tubular Zagato, was highly successful, but needed to evolve to stay competitive. Another two years on and the stunning TZ2 appeared, a lighter, more powerful and more modern-looking mini-GT, this time bodied in fibreglass – a radical departure for Zagato.

Powered by a modest, 170bhp, 1570cc straight-four, this was a small fish in a big pond, but with its low kerb weight, wind-cheating profile and kamm-tail design, the TZ2 could reach speeds in excess of 150mph.

1965 **Alfa Romeo GT Junior** ▼

Devised as an entry-level version of the bigger-bore GTV, Alfa's Giulia-based Junior soon became positively championed for its accessible simplicity. Affordable, tuneable, understated to behold but still a proper, rear-wheel drive GT, this was the people's car, Italian style.

Modest grunt came originally from an 89bhp, 1300cc, four-cylinder twin-cam but in 1972 a 1600cc engine was fitted with an extra 20bhp. It still wasn't particularly quick, but this was one of those rare cars that put a humble foot in the door of an exclusive and elusive world.

22 December 1965

The government announces the four-month trial of a new 70mph speed limit, which is still in place today – over 45 years later.

Although much maligned through the decades as the favoured steed of 'White Van Man', depicted filthy and dented with old copies of *The Sun* and empty sausage-roll wrappers spilling over the dashboard, the Ford Transit is, was and probably always will be an integral part of what makes Britain so British.

The first Transit was powerful, reliable and capable of taking a hammering. It was wider than the norm, too, making it much more spacious and, although it was primitive underneath, the sturdiness, comfort and handling prowess afforded by a wide-track, compact engine and rear-wheel drive was almost too good to be true. The Transit was sold in a variety of shapes and with a number of different engines, but the one everyone harks back to, and that probably contributed to that inauspicious reputation, was the massive 3.0-litre V6. Originally supplied to the emergency services, they were purportedly a must-have for getaway drivers at most 70s bank jobs.

8 February 1965

Mr and Mrs P. S. James are presented with the keys to their brand new Mini. Resplendent in white with a red interior, the car is the millionth Mini to be produced, driven off the Longbridge production line by Alec Issigonis himself. Mr and Mrs James won their Mini in a prize draw for BMC employees.

The first time the world clapped eyes on the stunning De Tomaso Sport 5000 was also pretty much the last. Designed as a barely legal GT racer, the V8 powered, Ghia-bodied spider was a one-off developed in close partnership with Caroll Shelby.

Well ahead of its time with a minimalist backbone chassis that incorporated its powerful, Ford-sourced engine as a stressed member, the design known internally as '70P' had all the right ingredients to become a major force on the sports-car circuit. But Shelby withdrew before the car was properly resolved and the final iteration of this stuttering project, by now referred to as the Ghia-De Tomaso Sport 5000, is believed to have broken down early on its debut and was never raced again.

All was not entirely lost, however, because the chassis and engine development was ploughed into the successful Mangusta road car. *Mangusta* is Italian for Mongoose, the only animal that eats Cobras...

1965 **Mini Marcos** ▼

Sold as a kit based on contemporary Mini running gear, the Mini Marcos was a miniscule, ultra-light and unspeakably ugly fibreglass club racer that won the world over by proving to be astonishingly fast and capable in the right hands. In 1966, in the turbulent slipstreams of mighty V12 and V8 adversaries from Porsche, Ferrari and Ford, a privateer Mini Marcos battled on to come 15th overall at Le Mans and was the only British car to finish that year. The French crowd nicknamed it Le Petite Puce – the little flea.

1966 **Saab Sonett II** ▼

After the faltering fancy of the first Sonett, Saab made a rather firmer fist of its second attempt in the mid-60s. This was a front-wheel drive, fibreglass-bodied, two-seat coupé with impressive handling and sprightly performance despite a tiny three-cylinder, two-stroke engine. Further evolutions included a larger, V4 1500cc unit from Ford and, in 1970, a sleeker Italian-inspired bodyshell to better appeal to the vital American market. It didn't really work, however and sales were slow despite some decent competition success. Fingers burned again, Saab pulled the plug in 1974 and hasn't built a two-seater since.

1966 **Chevrolet Camaro** ▶

Reacting to the runaway success of Ford's Mustang, GM launched the Chevrolet Camaro two years later. Following the now-proven format of mechanical simplicity and bags of grunt, it debuted with an entry-level straight-six and a dizzying array of increasingly large V8s. The first gen car only lasted three years before a restyle that hasn't been flattered by the passage of time, but those early cars have become as iconic and highly prized as the Mustang itself.

1966 **Fiat 124 Spider** ▶

A typically simple, yet effective effort from Italian styling gurus Pinifarina, the 124 Spider was not only designed but also made by them, using Fiat's running gear. This included an excellent, aluminium twin-cam engine that struck a hallowed balance between sturdiness and sportiness. Sadly, as was often the case in the 60s, the vast majority were sold to the US, making them rarer and more expensive on European soil than they really ought to be.

1966 **Ford Falcon XR GT** ▼

The Ford Falcon was, despite the name, Australia's answer to Britain's Cortina: a boring, workaday saloon for middle managers in brown suits. But mechanical associations with the Mustang encouraged Ford Down Under to offer a limited GT version using the same 4.7-litre, 225bhp V8 as its pony-car cousin. This, then, was the unlikely genesis of Australia's first muscle car, starting a cultural shift towards American V8s that dominates to this day.

1966 **Jensen Interceptor** ▶

A great 'What If?' in the annals of British motoring, the Jensen Interceptor steered close to stardom but somehow never quite made it. Powered by a whopping 325bhp, 6.3-litre, Chrysler V8, styled by Italian coachworks Touring and hand-built in Blighty, this was a practical, luxurious and fiercely fast GT. But production was slow, with only around 6,500 units appearing in almost 10 years.

1966 **Fiat Dino** ▼

Sold as both coupé and spyder, the Dino was a lesser, but not wholly unrelated, version of the Ferrari of the same name. Using the same 2.0-litre V6 as its sportier mid-engine counterpart, the Dino was practical, functional and hugely affordable by comparison.

Both styles are becoming increasingly collectible these days, especially the Pininfarina-styled drophead, but this remains the secret backdoor into classic Ferrari ownership, and all for the price of a Ford Focus.

12 January 1966

The jaws of a generation of schoolchildren collectively drop as Batman *debuts on television, complete with his now-infamous Batmobile. Painted bat-black with a blood-red trim, the Batmobile was based on a 1955 Lincoln Futura concept car, originally styled by Ghia in Turin.*

◄ 1966 **Ford Hertz Mustang**

In a bizarre act of seemingly suicidal marketing, Ford agreed to team up with rental giant Hertz to produce a series of Shelby-tuned Mustangs that it could loan out to the public. What went on in these cars is the stuff of legends, with Hertz Mustangs being entered into national racing events and even returned at the end of the day running a stock straight-six instead of the V8 with which it left the Hertz forecourt.

1966 **Ferrari 275 GTB** ▼

The 275 was the natural evolution of the 250 GTO, using the same 3.3-litre V12 in various states of tune. Not as pretty as the 250, it nevertheless offered significant engineering improvements and greater comfort for more viable grand-touring duties. An ultra-light Competitzione version was also built on an all-new chassis with tissue-thin aluminium bodywork. Suspiciously far removed from the road car, the GTB/C was nevertheless homologated and won its class at Le Mans in 1966 and 1967.

1966 **Porsche 911S**

The mid-60s was an unrivalled period for sports car manufacturing, giving rise to a higher proportion of design icons per square foot of factory floor than at any other time in the whole of motoring history. But perhaps the greatest single product of this prolific purple patch was the Porsche 911.

Evolving Ferry Porsche's original concept of the 356, with its rear-mounted, air-cooled flat-four, the 1963 911 provided more interior space, more comfort, more power from its larger, 2.0-litre flat-six, and preternatural handling. Three years later the high performance 'S' appeared, regarded by many as the consummate sporting GT. Subtle but skilful engine modifications increased the power output by 20 per cent to 160bhp, giving an already quick road car a turn of speed normally reserved for the circuit. But this was still a highly driveable and functional compact 2+2 that, while expensive, significantly undercut exotic Italian and British fare from the period.

The original 911S was a tricky bugger, with a tendency towards snap oversteer at the limit. Porsche lengthened the wheelbase after a couple of white-knuckle years and things were marginally improved, but the 911's weight distribution remained a challenge on road and track.

Nevertheless, this is the car that has dominated sports car racing like no other, winning countless races on every continent in professional and amateur hands for decade upon decade. Reliable, tuneable, fast and, relative to the excrutiating cost of going racing, quite cheap to campaign, this is the ultimate evocation of Ferdinand Porsche's inspired democratic vision, begun with the Beetle back in the 30s.

1966 **Jaguar XJ13** ▶

Jaguar's still-born Le Mans project is perhaps the ultimate might-have-been in British sports car history. Here was a mid-engine V12 with aviation-grade aerodynamics, built specifically to put the wind up Ferrari and Porsche on the international sports-car circuit. It was gob-smackingly beautiful, fast and, to a point, superb to drive. Unfortunately, development was under-funded and consequently slow. By the time it was ready to race, the more advanced Ford GT40 was lording it up at Le Mans. The XJ13 was deemed old hat and mothballed.

1966 **Lotus Europa** ▼

The Europa was a curious-looking car, thanks in part to racing roots that put aesthetics behind aerodynamics. The first road-going Lotus to benefit from a mid-engined configuration, most cars were fitted with cheap and robust 1.5-litre Renault engines, graduating to a more powerful but typically tricky Lotus twin-cam in the early 70s. The Europa stayed true to Chapman's essential engineering principles with a steel backbone and fibreglass monocoque. It weighed almost nothing and out-handled absolutely everything. Tick in the box.

1966 **Alfa Romeo Duetto Spider** ▼

The Duetto was a stroke of genius by Alfa Romeo, combining simple, elegant lines with tried-and-tested mechanicals to create an object of practical beauty. Styled and built by Pininfarina and powered originally by Alfa's 1.6-litre twin cam, this wasn't a fast nor particularly involving car to drive, but its masterstroke was in selling the mid-60s Italian dream to the world. And in continuing to sell it in subtly revised guises right up until the early 90s, long after the dream had sold up, bought a Vauxhall and moved into a gated community.

1966 **De Tomaso Mangusta** ▶

With just over 400 units ever built, the Mangusta was Big Time for Alejandro De Tomaso. Designed by Giugiaro and driven by a 4.7-litre Ford V8 mounted amidships, this was a beautiful and powerful thing, made all the more desirable by that limited availability.

With speeds in excess of 150mph theoretically achievable, the Mangusta might have been a real supercar contender, but Alejandro De Tomaso hadn't reckoned on the laws of physics. The Mangusta's near 70/30 weight distribution made it absolutely lethal.

1966 **Lamborghini Miura** ▼

The myth behind the Miura is appositely romantic: while founder Ferruccio was concentrating on building fast but luxurious grand tourers, some of his engineers spent their downtime coming up with an out-and-out sports car, complete with mid-engine V12, noisy two-seat cockpit and the sort of styling that would snap knicker elastic at a thousand paces. Early cars were reported to experience terrifying front-end lift as the fuel tank emptied, but this was a mere peccadillo. The public went wild for it and production began within a year, reshaping Lamborghini's design direction forever.

1966 **Maserati Ghibli** ▶

The Maserati Ghibli was a thoroughly modern product when it first emerged in 1966. The firm's iconic but ageing twin-spark straight-six was a thing of the past and beneath the long, Ghia-designed, Corvette-alike bonnet, a 330bhp 4.7-litre V8 now burbled. Infamously thirsty, the Ghibli got through so much fuel that Maserati were forced to fit two 50-litre tanks, but this didn't stop it becoming a bestseller that stayed in production for almost seven years.

1966 **Ferrari 330 GTC** ▶

Sharing its underpinnings and 3.3-litre V12 with the 275 GTB, the 330 GTC was a compact two-seat road-going sports car that dispensed with the touring pretensions of the 330 GT 2+2.

A shorter wheelbase made this a more involving driver, and in many respects this was the last real link to the sprightly 250's racing heyday, before the tank-like 365 Daytona brought Ferrari and its customers into a new era.

1966 **Bizzarrini 5300 Strada** ▼

Having parted company with Iso Rivolta, former Ferrari engine guru Giotto Bizzarrini set about making his own V12 two-seater, using most of the ideas he had forged for racing the Iso Grifo. The 5300 Strada is a stunning legacy for Bizzarrini's mid-60s magic, with its curvaceous and distinctly phallic aluminium Bertone bodywork and race-bred V12. Impossibly cramped despite its vast proportions and hopelessly high maintenance to boot, this was part of a dying breed of competition-focussed road-going exotica. Play things of the mega rich, then and now.

1967 **Alfa Romeo Tipo 33 Stradale** ▶

Based on the 33 Tipo racecar, the Stradale, meaning 'street going', was re-bodied by Franco Scaglione and slightly detuned. But its mid-mounted, 2.0-litre V8 still made 230bhp – plenty for a 700kg kerbweight. The 33s were legendary racecars but all are eclipsed by the beauty of Scaglione's symphony of curves.

1967 **Mercury Cougar** ▼

Another one of those American muscle cars that got progressively more awful as the decades ticked by, the Mercury Cougar started out superbly as a re-bodied Ford Mustang. It was larger and slightly more luxurious, but the mechanical underpinnings were the same. Things stayed largely unchanged until 1974 when the third gen Cougar appeared on a larger, less sporty platform, apparently styled for pimps in felt hats and brothel creepers.

1967 **Matra M530** ▼

Matra was a small French racing firm with impressive showings in Formula 1 and at Le Mans. Its road cars were few and far between, however, with the most successful being the M530. This was a modestly powered, mid-engined, two-seater with a Targa top and brave, angular styling.

Made of fibreglass and powered by Ford's Taunus V4, the M530 was intended to be cheap and cheerful and the car's fit and finish betrayed this. But with relatively sophisticated suspension and fine handling balance, the essence of Matra's racing expertise was now available to Joe Public at a bargain price.

7 April 1967

John Lennon takes delivery of a Rolls-Royce, complete with psychedelic yellow paint work. Legend has it that as the Beatle drove through the streets of London he was attacked by an elderly woman screaming, "You swine! You swine! How dare you do this to a Rolls-Royce!"

1967 **Ginetta G15** ▶

In keeping with Ginetta's philosophy of affordable thrills, the G15 was designed as a road-going kit car with competition potential. A simple chassis and compact fibreglass body housed a mildly tuned engine from the Hillman Imp. But this, in turn, was a revised version of the Le Mans-winning Coventry Climax unit, so the scope for serious performance upgrades was almost limitless.

The G15 was beautifully balanced and, when appropriately fettled, was also impressively fast. In privateer hands the little Ginetta was regularly found showing far pricier factory fare from Lotus a clean pair of heels.

1967 **Lancia Fulvia Sport Zagato** ▶

With curious styling and a slightly ungainly stance, the Lancia Fulvia Sport was a bit love-it-or-hate-it from the off. But it was also by far the cheapest way to get into Zagato ownership. The standard coupé was re-bodied in angular aluminium by the distinctive and avant-garde coachbuilders. Lancia's front-wheel drive chassis and buzzy, 1.3-litre V4 engine still ensured it was a great little driver's car, but now you had the added benefit – if you saw it that way – of being clothed by perhaps the most prestigious automotive tailor around.

1967 **Toyota 2000 GT** ▼

Hugely significant for being the car that made the world sit up and pay attention to the Japanese motoring industry, Toyota's 2000 GT was a major national milestone. Gracefully shaped in aluminium and powered by a twin-cam, straight-six, this was a fast and fine-handling sports car that put the frighteners on Europe's big boys. Today, Japanese collectors fight tooth-and-nail to own these scarce, pricey pieces of home-grown heritage.

1967 **NSU Ro80** ▶

When it first appeared in the dark ages of three-box saloon motoring, the NSU Ro80, with its rotary engine, refinement, sophistication and handling prowess, was like a thing from another world.

Stylish, superbly made and simply light years ahead of the sort of thing your average British family were banging about in, it was worth every penny of its massive ticket price. Until the rotary engines started going terminally wrong, usually well inside 10,000 miles. NSU honoured warranty after warranty until it was effectively bankrupted and bought out by Volkswagen. Oops.

◀ 1967 **Aston Martin DBS**

As Aston continues to plunder its heritage to please footballers and their many wives, little-known gems like the original DBS are all but forgotten. Far from the cynical bling of the revamped DB9 that is currently touting the moniker, the first DBS was a subtle and modest gentleman's GT. A radical styling evolution over the DB6 it replaced, the 'S' used the same engine, originally in a detuned state, and had proper rear seats for added practicality. Destined for V8 power and increasingly macho styling alterations, the DBS was the last of David Brown's elegant, understated straight-sixes.

1967 **Monteverdi High Speed 375S** ▼

With the exception of penknives and watches, there aren't many Swiss exports to get excited about. But things were rather different in 1967 when Peter Monteverdi introduced the High Speed 375S. This was an elegant, massive, powerful, two-seat coupé, designed by Pietro Frua and built in Basel of all places. Solidly finished and exquisitely appointed, this was high-speed, high-end luxury transport at its finest.

1967 **Ferrari 330P4** ▶

Ask a child of the seventies to draw his ultimate sports car and chances are that the unfettered imagination of youth would conjure up something not unlike the Ferrari P4. Built to take part in endurance races like Le Mans and Daytona, the P4 was a stunning example of how aerodynamics unites form and function. It was also the car that exacted Enzo's revenge on the mighty GT40s by completing a 1,2,3 finish on Ford's home soil at Daytona.

◀ 1967 **Lotus 49**

The 49 was one of the great British Formula 1 cars, establishing various design precedents that are still in evidence today. It won its inaugural race in the hands of Jim Clark and took the World Championship the following year with team-mate Graham Hill. It was Colin Chapman's genius that was central, however, with the 49's chassis and engine set-up becoming a pivotal point in the evolution of F1.

1967 **Shelby Mustang GT500** ▼

Considered by many to be the ultimate evocation of the Mustang, the Shelby GT 500 was powered by the final evolution of Ford's mighty FE V8, the 350bhp 428 'Police Interceptor'. Although by this point the engineering influence of Shelby American was taking a back seat, its raw, race-hewn focus was evident in every detail of the 500's running gear. Today, the original GT500s are regarded as the jewel in Ford's post-war crown.

1967 **Zil 114** ▶

Zavod imeni Likhachova, or Zil for short, is a Russian manufacturer of heavy-duty kit-like trucks and military vehicles that also has a line in limousines. Back in the late 60s these were almost all for Politburo members and many were heavily armoured.

The Zil was seriously luxurious for Soviet-era Russia, featuring early versions of air conditioning and heat deflecting glass. Nearly 6.5 metres long and weighing over 3 tonnes, its homegrown 300bhp V8 still got car and comrades to over 100mph.

◀ 1968 **Citroën Mehari**

The Mehari was a plastic-bodied, no-nonsense runabout built for nearly 20 years by Citroën. Based on the mumsy Dyane, which itself was based on the sardine tin 2CV, the Mehari was the boys' toys alternative.

Incredibly basic exactly when you wanted it to be, the Mehari was easy to fix, delighted to get dirty and surprisingly good at crossing terrible terrain thanks to a minimal kerbweight and relatively good ground clearance. It looked like shit, but you weren't supposed to care.

13 August 1967

Warren Beatty and Faye Dunaway star in Bonnie and Clyde, *driving their stolen Ford V8 B400 all the way to two Academy Awards.*

1968 **Volkswagen Baja Bug** ▶

An unofficial VW product, the Baja Bug first appeared in California where larking about in the desert was a burgeoning motoring trend for young, sun-soaked petrolheads with more space and more petrol than they could possibly cope with.

Taking its inspiration from the Meyers Manx, but using stock Beetle bodyshells, the Bajas were jacked up on huge tyres and suspension systems and then tweaked into ridiculous states of tune. As entertaining as they were lethal when rolled off a vertical sand dune, the Baja Bugs are part of the very fabric of Californian car culture.

1968 **Marcos Mantis XP** ▶

Taking West Country carpentry into the big leagues of sportscar racing, Marcos fitted a contemporary Formula 1 engine to the plywood chassis of its Mantis XP, and then shrouded this bizarre union in an equally unlikely plastic skin.

Sadly it only raced once, at the Spa 1000KM in Belgium, and threw in the towel early due to an electrical glitch. But surrounded on the grid by sensual 60s curves, its visionary angular bodywork and gull-wing doors made entirely of plexiglass made this one of the most startling and memorable creations of the decade.

1968 **Ferrari Dino 206 GT** ▼

The origins of the Dino are found in Enzo's son Alfredo, who died aged 24. 'Alfredino' had wanted his father to build a V6 for smaller, more affordable cars, an idea Ferrari pursued with the front-engined Fiat Dino in '66 and the Dino 206GT two years later.

The cars were marketed as Dinos in order to distinguish them from their more exclusive and expensive V12 stablemates, but the superbly balanced and beautiful 206 has since become one of the most sought-after Italian sports cars and is now regarded as a Ferrari through and through.

1968 **Opel GT** ▶

Opel is the European parent of Vauxhall, there to make sensible cars for sensible people in sensible shoes. But it has enjoyed the occasional foray into desirability, the best of which is the late-60s 'GT.'

Although the power going to its rear wheels was really only noticeable by its absence (67bhp in the entry-level car, rising to 100bhp if you splashed out on the flagship single cam 1.9-litre) the styling had echoes of contemporary Corvettes and even the Ferrari Daytona. Nothing if not ambitious.

1968 **Lamborghini Espada** ▶

One of the major stumbling blocks of sports car design has always been incorporating a proper rear row of seats without bodging both appearance and performance. And the Espada, Lamborghini's mighty V12 GT, was as close as anyone got to solving the problem for the next 40 years.

Sold alongside the two-seat '400' and mid-engine Miura, the Espada was undeniably weird-looking but, with the capacity to seat four adults and shift them at speeds in excess of 150mph, was some achievement for the late 60s. Testament to its practical appeal, the Espada comfortably outsold its stablemates, staying in production for a decade.

◀ 1968 **Lamborghini Islero**

The little-known successor to Lamborghini's 400 GT, the Islero highlights a gradual shift in Italy's coachworks industry from the curvaceous bodywork of the 60s to their more angular output in the 70s.

The Islero was a still very much a 60s GT underneath, however, with a 2+2 seating configuration and front-engine V12 sending over 340bhp to the rear. But it enjoyed various subtle mechanical and interior changes that made it easier to live with and better to drive. This was, however, the beginning of the end for Lamborghini's GT production, with attention now turning to impractical but more desirable mid-engined sports cars.

1968 **Ferrari Daytona** ▶

Officially designated the 365 GTB/4, the Daytona was a bold departure for Ferrari with its uncharacteristic angles penned by Pininfarina. An evolution of the 275GTB's V12 burbled under that vast, sharp-nosed bonnet, meaning that, despite the slow speed impression of steering a cargo ship, once up and at it the Daytona felt remarkably light and agile.

With 352bhp on tap and a record-breaking 174mph possible, this was the fastest production car on sale.

1968 **Dodge Charger** ▼

Despite first appearing in 1966 it was the restyled second Charger, unveiled two years later, that really captured the American imagination and went on to become one of the definitive outlines in muscle-car history.

A classic product of the Motor City heyday, the Charger was an agricultural bit of kit with increasingly vast V8 engines appearing year on year, the ultimate option being the R/T, short for Road/Track.

These cars were equipped with a 375bhp Magnum V8, uprated brakes and a handling pack. And for an extra $600 you could order up the 426 Hemi engine, taking power up to a ridiculous 425bhp. Needless to say, an awful lot of people did.

1969 Ford Capri 3.0-litre ▼

With Ford in the US selling every Mustang before the paint was dry, its European arm came up with its own local alternative. The Capri Mk 1 was a skilfully slimmed-down take on the original pony car, with a proper fast back design and front-engine, rear-wheel drive layout. Although sold with a variety of weedy engines to make it attainable for the working man, Ford's UK division also produced a 138bhp, 3.0-litre V6 which gave it a more respectable turn of speed and some suitably alarming handling characteristics. This was a rough-and-ready car, not always brilliantly built and certainly not great to drive, but somehow this just added to hairy-chested, blue-collar charm.

1969 Bristol 411 ▶

As the decade of sexual revolution and political upheaval drew to a close, nothing much was changing at Bristol Cars.

Still producing large, odd-looking and horrifically expensive gentlemen's grand tourers, stoutly stuck together around gigantically thirsty Chrysler V8s and slushy three-speed auto boxes, Bristol was performing a vital public service in reassuring an older, more recalcitrant generation that although their daughters might be living in sin with state-educated communists who listened to reggae, the world had yet to go entirely to the dogs.

Bristol kept up this charade for another 40 years.

Built in small numbers for privateer racing, the Chevron B16 was one of those plucky upstarts that came out of nowhere to thrash the established opposition.

Designed by a man called Derek Bennett, the B16 featured a reinforced tubular spaceframe and light, low, beautiful fibreglass bodywork. With a 1600cc Cosworth engine strapped on, the B16 went out and won its debut at the Nürburgring in 1969.

Orders flooded in despite a lack of development that meant the car was still suffering from near-terminal understeer, a flaw that had been hidden at the race by the considerable skills of Chevron's works driver Brian Redman.

18 June 1969

The balance of power shifts in Italy, as Fiat purchases a 50% stake in Ferrari, enabling Enzo and co. more financial muscle to commission, develop and market their road cars.

1969 Triumph TR6 ▼

The last of the truly collectible Triumphs, the TR6 was a sort of mini muscle car in its own right with a throaty, 2.5-litre straight-six and rear-wheel drive. This was old school stuff by the end of the 60s though, with its steel body panels bolted to a separate chassis and four-speed manual with overdrive available as an option.

But with independent suspension and disc brakes up front, the TR6 was still a decent driver's car, offering impressive performance for its price.

It also boasted early, and not exactly brilliant, fuel injection but the American market, where the overwhelming majority were sold, opted for a detuned version on carbs. Which was probably quite sensible.

Nowadays people have twigged that the TR6 was the final hurrah for Triumph Proper, and that this underrated two-seater has all the qualities of a truly classic British roadster. Prices are on the up for a slice of our former glories.

1969 Peugeot 504 Cabriolet ▶

What makes the 504 Cabriolet quite so special is the fact that, in all honesty, it shouldn't be anything of the sort. A late-60s Peugeot built at a time of industrial strife in the French car industry, with little in the way of oomph and a propensity to rust, the 504 had all the makings of a complete turd. So it's testament to the unpredictable brilliance of our continental cousins that both coupé and elegant drop-top were instantly recognised for their good qualities and remain highly sought after to this day.

The 504 had excellent road manners, finding the right balance between comfort and handling to be a brisk and refined little sports tourer, and its styling, understated but attractive, was the perfect compliment. Forty years on, Peugeot has yet to better it.

1970s
THE MORNING AFTER

This was to be a decade of confusion and introspection, with much of the blinkered optimism of the 60s giving way to scepticism and anger. America was embittered after a decade of pot smoking and casual sex had given them little more than Vietnam and a crook in the Whitehouse. And to make matters worse, they had to tolerate it all while wearing bell-bottoms.

The Cold War was cracking along nicely too, and unrest in the Middle East was still something you could set your watch by. This took its most catastrophic turn for the motoring industry in the shape of the 1973 oil crisis, which saw the price of petrol sky-rocket and stay there. The effect was devastating, with small sports-car companies hammered into bankruptcy almost overnight and thirsty new supercars abandoned in their infancy. The institutional US gas-guzzler never quite recovered and the small, economical Japanese alternative began its inexorable global rise.

On home soil, things weren't particularly groovy any more, either. This was the decade of strikes, with miners, postmen and bin-men all forming picket lines and the three-day week imposed to save energy. Glam rock was the big thing, with David Bowie and Elton John mincing about in spandex while Marc Bolan hitched a ride in his girlfriend's Mini.

He might have been better off in an MGB. This was the period when everyone had one; no wonder there was a national malaise setting in. Today people only seem to talk about the long hot summer of '76 in terms of how close they came to dying of thirst. Which, according to government figures on the water level in August, was 'very'.

There was hope, however. And we're not talking about the Queen's Jubilee. This was the decade that would bring us the Golf GTI, the ultimate all-rounder, and the legendarily lethal Porsche 911 Turbo. More miraculous yet, Lancia would rock the World Rally scene with the Ferrari-powered Stratos and TVR would stay solvent. The 60s this was not, but there was still fun to be had if you knew where to look.

1970 **Alfa Romeo Montreal** ▼

The Montreal was something of an oddity for Alfa Romeo. Its American muscle car looks were out of character for starters, as was naming it after a Canadian city. That was one of those tail-wagging-dog moments, however, since Alfa had chosen to unveil their unnamed concept car in Montreal in 1967 and a smitten media nicknamed it after the city.

In many respects this was still Alfa of old though, based largely on the live-axle Guilia platform (like everything else it made) and styled by Bertone. But up front was a race-derived and rev-happy, 2.6-litre V8 that gave the Montreal a serious head of steam. This was a light, agile and rapid 2+2 that was really only held back by a wickedly steep ticket price.

1970 **Dodge Challenger** ▶

Taking the Mustang's pony-car concept up a notch, the Dodge Challenger was devised to provide similar levels of brutal straight-line speed, but with a greater focus on space and comfort.

Offered with an enormous array of parent company Chrysler's engines, the entry-level Challenger's 3.0-litre straight-six would swell into a monstrous 7.0-litre V8 at the top of the range. But the one to have was the T/A, for Trans Am, finished with a matt-black fibreglass bonnet and gigantic power bulge. This was a homologation special with uprated suspension and greater power. Painted in garish colours and a terrible handful to drive, the Challenger T/A was as brash and ostentatious as muscle cars got. And that's saying something.

1970 Porsche 914 ▶

The 914 was a curious joint project between Porsche and Volkswagen, using VW parts wherever possible to keep costs down, including the firm's modest but reliable flat-four. Porsche also began selling a version with a flat-six taken from its 911 but it was a pricey non-starter. Most 914s went to the States, in particular California where the climate suited its Targa top and propensity to rust.

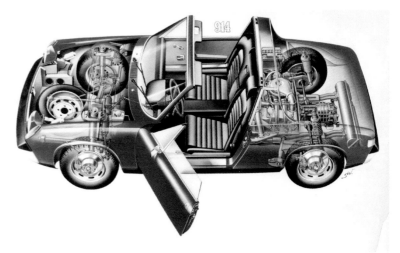

1970 Toyota Celica ▼

The original Celica was the first mass-production sports GT from Japan, taking on from where the far pricier and more exclusive 2000 GT had left off. Its styling had obvious echoes of contemporary American muscle cars but it was a small car with small engines and an accordingly small price tag. The Celica was a great drive though, and the 1600cc GT began what was to become one of the great rally success stories of the next three decades.

The Stag was a departure for Triumph. While still building its two-seat TR6 roadster, the seeds were sown for an unlikely four-seat open tourer based on the humdrum 2000 saloon but powered by a V8. It was a radical idea back then and still is today, but somehow it really worked. The critical issue of styling was taken care of by long-term Triumph and Maserati collaborator Giovanni Michelotti, while the 3.0-litre V8 power was designed and built in-house. This was less of a success, with reliability problems dogging early Stags, and it soon became common practise for owners to swap in sturdier Rover and Ford engines.

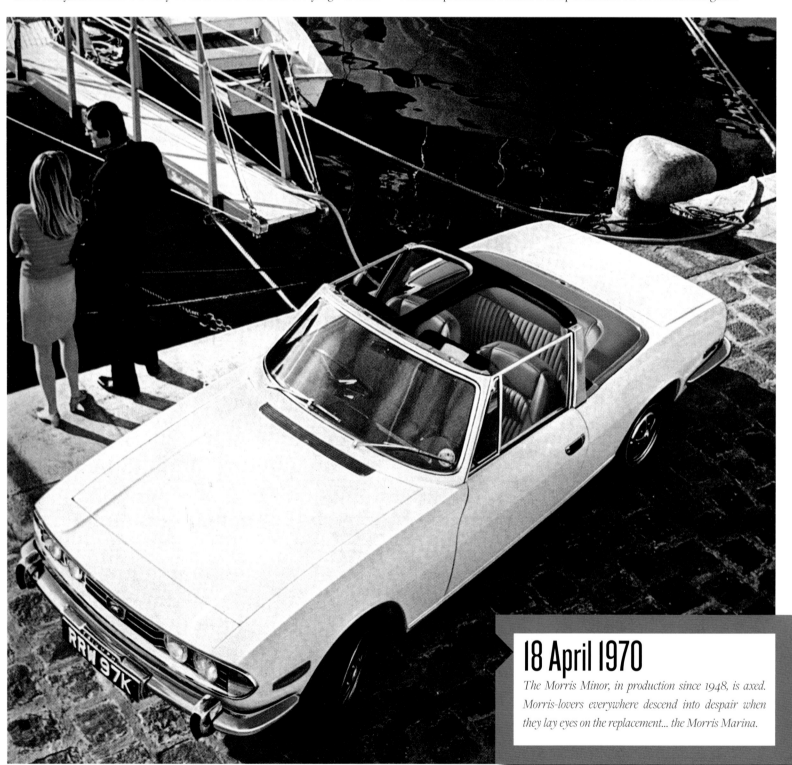

18 April 1970

The Morris Minor, in production since 1948, is axed. Morris-lovers everywhere descend into despair when they lay eyes on the replacement... the Morris Marina.

1970 **Plymouth Barracuda** ▶

It was in 1970 that the Barracuda found its stride when Plymouth dispensed with the smaller chassis of its 60s models and built up an all-new model on the 'E-Body' platform. This was shared with the Dodge Challenger, and the Barracuda followed a similar theme of capacious luxury and absurd levels of power. Less popular than the Challenger when new, the scarcity of the Barracuda today makes it even hotter property.

1970 **Citroën SM** ▶

Having bought out the financially stricken Maserati in 1968, Citroën set about exploiting its newly acquired asset by pinching a high-performance V6 engine. Typically bonkers, the SM was a front-wheel drive luxury GT-cum-estate with air suspension and all sorts of elaborate gimmicks like headlights that turned with the steering wheel. It wasn't all show, however. The SM was quick and out-handled far more established sports cars of the era.

1970 **Ford Torino** ▶

Although mass-produced as a boring mid-sized family saloon and estate car, the Torino everyone remembers is a chest-thumping muscle car. Ford shoehorned its 7.0-litre V8 into the Torino Cobra, gave it a short-shift, four-speed gearbox and took out any unnecessary luxuries. The result was a devastatingly quick little coupé that could out-drag the best that its Motor City rivals had to offer.

1970 **Ferrari 512 S** ▼

With homologation requirements meaning Ferrari had way more 512 S racing chassis than it knew what to do with, Enzo gave one of the last to Pininfarina and said: "Knock yourself out". In Italian.

The result is perhaps one of the most outlandish but effective concept cars ever created, a near-perfect 70s vision of the supercar future, albeit a future where you can't actually turn the front wheels.

Japan's fascination with all things miniature reached its auto industry at an early stage and by 1970 Honda had turned out the first micro sports coupé, the Z600.

It was absolutely tiny and made whoever drove it look like an idiot. But then the oil crisis arrived and the Z's staggering fuel economy made it the envy of every Aston and Ferrari owner in the land. Small was suddenly very cool.

1970 **Audi 100 S** ▶

Considering its relative obscurity, the original Audi 100 is an enormously important car. Designed in the wings at parent company Volkswagen while the Beetle was still flying out of showrooms, this was the car that accurately forecast an impending global demand for affordable, reliable, water-cooled front-engine cars. The 100 S Coupé was elegant and entertaining to drive but it was also modern and eminently practical. Here was the future, and it was all German.

1970 **Datsun 240Z** ▼

Known as the Fairlady in Japan and the 240Z in the US, and either a Datsun or a Nissan depending on who you were talking to, the original 'Zed' was a highpoint for Japanese sports car manufacture.

Well balanced, with sophisticated suspension and reasonable poke, it outclassed various well-established European rivals and did it for a lot less money.

1970 **Plymouth Superbird** ▶

In many ways the final evolution of the original muscle car, the Plymouth Superbird was an utterly ridiculous road-legal NASCAR racer that, with its drooping aerodynamic nosecone and gigantic rear wing, looked like it had been designed by Warner Bros. Made for one year only for homologation purposes, the 425bhp V8 Superbird was as fast as it was absurd and is now one of the highest prizes for mega-wealthy collectors of Detroit metal.

1970 **Range Rover** ▶

The Land Rover as we know it first appeared in the late 40s, providing rugged and basic off-road transport for soldier and civvy alike. For years afterwards, the bigwigs at Rover were eyeing a gap in the market for a more road-oriented offering, still with impressive all-terrain ability, but providing greater space, comfort and refinement.

When the original Range Rover appeared it was considerably more sophisticated than its contemporary, with coil springs, a V8 and, over time, increasing levels of luxury.

In the days before they became a status symbol for the perma-tanned nouveau-riche, the muddy three-door Range Rover was a class act: honest and functional, full of wet dogs and weekly shops, keeping Middle England moving.

1970 **Pontiac Firebird Trans Am** ▼

Another of America's seemingly endless stream of mechanically identical muscle cars, the Firebird was a GM working-class hero in the traditional vein: cheap, simple, powerful. In 1970 the second gen car was launched with more distinctive styling and, although arguably less pretty than the first, it was this look that established the Firebird in popular culture. The model everyone aspired to was the Trans Am, with its meaty and sonorous, 7.5-litre V8. US-emissions limits were tightening on such indulgencies, however, meaning this would be one of the last proper pony cars.

1970 **Porsche 917** ▶

For devotees of Porsche or bygone Le Mans, there is no single racing car more significant or evocative than the 917. Designed to take Porsche's first outright win at Le Mans, the 917 was a wildly expensive development project featuring ground-breaking ideas like pressurizing the hollow spaceframe with gas to both strengthen it and reveal any weakness.

With a highly complicated and powerful 12-cylinder engine developing unprecedented speeds in sports car racing, the 917 was a fearsome handful. Aerodynamic revisions brought Porsche the Le Mans crown they were after in both 1970 and '71, the latter win also witnessing a 246mph top speed and the fastest lap ever recorded there.

1970 **Ford Escort Mexico** ▶

Ford in the 70s was the Working Man's domain, all big 'taches, real ale and rallying. In order to cash in on its competition success in the London-to-Mexico rally, Ford produced the Mexico, with underpinnings from the sportier RS and a detuned 86bhp engine. It instantly gained blue-collar cult status thanks to hairy rear-wheel drive handling, spot lamps and go-faster stripes. It was a bit rubbish really, but that's a vital part of its charm.

1970 **Monteverdi Hai** ▶

Evolving much like Lamborghini, albeit without really selling cars, Peter Monteverdi also abandoned his fast and luxurious GT in favour of a mid-engine supercar. And so, too, did his new project feature highly contemporary angular styling and a massive displacement V8 behind the seats.

The Hai was to have been as expensive as it was fast, and it is probably for this reason that production never made it beyond two prototypes.

1 June 1970

Legendary coachbuilders Ghia of Turin, designers of iconic cars for Fiat, Alfa Romeo and Lancia among others, is acquired by Ford.

1971 Land Rover III Station Wagon

The final evolution of the original, proper, Land Rover, the Series III arguably strikes the best balance between adherence to the (very) basic concept and concessions to the demands of modern motoring. Which is still 'virtually none'.

But this was the flat-pack off-roader, simple to ship to every corner of the globe, simple to build up on arrival and rebuild when it broke, which they invariably did. The majority of Land Rovers ever made are still on the road today, though, suggesting that something doesn't even need to be good to be great.

What makes the Station Wagon the definitive Landie is that Safari roof, a clever ventilated twin-skin design that insulated the interior in winter and cooled it in summer. In theory, at least. The roof may have been a bit hit and miss, but then so were Land Rovers, and it gives the Station Wagon a colonial authenticity and undeniably romantic purpose.

1971 **Alfa Romeo Alfasud** ▶

Styled by Giugiaro, powered by a characterful little flat-four engine and blessed with preternaturally good handling, the Alfasud was destined for greatness. Practical, affordable and a hoot to drive, the compact but spacious 'Sud only weighed 830kg, enabling its meagre 63bhp to achieve a respectable 93mph.

There was, however, an Achilles' Heel: rust. Succumbing to the elements like no Alfa before or since, the original and comparatively high-volume 'Sud is now something of a rarity.

1971 **Maserati Bora** ▶

Keen to keep abreast of Lamborghini and its ilk, Maserati decided to take a stab at the mid-engine, two-seat, supercar market. Sold alongside its established and proven front-engined Ghibli tourer, the Bora appeared in 1971 with the same 4.7-litre V8, this time wedged behind the driver.

What sets the Bora apart is that it was designed and built to offer a more comfortable, refined and sophisticated alternative to standard Italian exotica. The engine bay was heavily sound insulated, the glass double-glazed. This sort of thing made it heavier and therefore slower than the competition – but after 165mph who's counting?

1971 **Alpine A310** ▶

The successor to the World Rally Championship winning A110, Alpine's A310 followed a similar configuration of steel backbone chassis, fibreglass body and Renault-sourced engine precariously bolted beyond the rear axle. Although not blessed with the competition success of its predecessor, the A310 looks fantastic and, when upgraded to a 2.7-litre V6 in 1976, went like stink.

1971 De Tomaso Pantera ▼

The mid-engine, V8 Pantera is the car that defines De Tomaso in the public consciousness. Its exquisite shape, effortlessly balancing elegance with real sporting menace, stole many a heart back in 1971 and continued to do so right into the early 90s. The Pantera was quick, luxurious by the standards of the day and highly exclusive due to the slow, hand-built production line.

But those hands were not as skilled as De Tomaso would have wanted, and the Pantera earned a reputation for being atrociously made. This reached its public relations nadir in a legendary incident when Elvis Presley, despairing of his bright yellow Pantera's refusal to start, shot it with a pistol on the drive at Graceland.

31 July 1971

Apollo 15 Commander David Scott becomes the first motorist on the moon when he gets behind the wheel of the Lunar Rover.

1971 **Mercedes-Benz 450 SLC** ▶

Celebrated as being one of the last truly classic Mercs, the SLC was a large, luxurious and bomb-proof V8 coupé. On sale for a decade, during which time few revisions were made to a near foolproof product, the SLC was essentially a longer version of the pretty but less practical SL roadster, offering an extended wheelbase to house useable rear seats.

But its finest hour came in the unlikely guise of a factory rally version which, making full use of performance improvements like a lightweight 5.0-litre V8 and aluminium body panels, was campaigned with remarkable success around the world.

1971 **Buick Riviera** ▼

By now in its third iteration with elegant Corvette-alike 'boat-tail' rear styling, the 5.5-metre long Buick Riviera was a mighty two-door coupé continuing the theme of 'Personal Luxury' started by the Ford Thunderbird. This remained a euphemism for dynamic incompetence, but that was seldom a problem in the US where the Riviera's point-and-squirt driving style, made all the more unconvincing by a lumbering, 7.5-litre V8, was just what the greying, change-resistant muscle car buyers of the 60s now wanted.

1972 De Tomaso Longchamp ▶

A bizarre and little-known stablemate of the famous Pantera, De Tomaso's Longchamp coupé was a far subtler, front-engined, 2+2 offering greater luxury and practicality in a more approachable dynamic package.

Although built in very low volume right up until the end of the 80s, the thirsty, V8-engined Longchamp's timing was terrible, with the 1973 oil crisis causing sales to stall in those vital early years.

1972 Fiat 126 ▶

The Fiat 500 had been in production for almost 20 years and was overripe for replacement. The boxy, less loveably styled 126 that did the job in hand followed the same format of small, four-seat family transport with an air-cooled engine – an enlarged version the 500's in fact – in the boot.

But there was something rather special about the 126: it drove like a dream. Built in Italy and Poland, where production only stopped in 2000, the functional and affordable shopping cart was an absolute diamond around Europe's winding city streets where its rear-wheel drive and excellent traction made it far faster and more agile than its artless outline would have you believe.

◀ 1972 Ferrari Daytona Shooting Brake

One-off cars are a bit pointless, in that they're usually commissioned by immensely wealthy Sheiks and squirreled away in airtight garages, never again to see the light of day. Happily the Ferrari Daytona Shooting Brake has been gamely paraded around the US and Europe for years, where its mini-estate dimensions, with glass rear hatch and hinged gull-wing canopies, can be fully appreciated for the stroke of loony genius that it is. Destroying a perfectly good Daytona and rebuilding it as a warp-speed dad wagon was a travesty of near-criminal proportions, but somehow the inspired and deeply 70s Shooting Brake completely got away with it.

One of the more curious collaborations in British sports car history – and that's saying something – the Jensen-Healey was designed in conjunction with the Austin family, built by Jensen of Interceptor fame and powered by a Lotus twin-cam engine. All of which did not really add up to the sum of its parts. Striking looking but indifferently finished and prone to both major mechanical catastrophe and rust, the Jensen-Healey was a near miss that, like so many cars of its time, was cut down before its prime by the oil crisis.

Today they have garnered a small but loyal following, all exceptionally busy maintaining early 70s Lotus engines and keeping round-the-clock corrosion vigil.

17 February 1972

Henry Ford Loses out to Adolf Hitler as Adolf's 'people's car', the Volkswagen Beetle, surpasses the production record of Henry's Model T when the 15,007,034th Beetle scuttles off the production line.

1972 **TVR 1600M** ▶

With its fortunes flailing, TVR's M-Series was introduced by new boss Martin Lilley to improve upon the outdated Vixen. The cars were still fibreglass-bodied two-seaters but with a simpler, tougher, square-tube chassis onto which a variety of domestic engines could be bolted.

The period, moustachioed TVR buyer favoured the 2.5 and 3.0-litre, six-cylinder options over the slower 1600M with its 1588cc Ford four-pot, and within a year the entry-level M was dropped. But then the 1973 oil crisis took hold and TVR reintroduced it to a chastened sports car market. Suddenly its superior weight distribution and fine handling balance were being celebrated rather more.

1972 **Lancia Stratos** ▼

Originally a styling exercise that was taken more seriously than Bertone expected, the svelte and futuristic Stratos concept was seized upon by Lancia's competition department as a glamorous and innovative route to sporting stardom.

Developed for the World Rally Championship, the plastic-bodied, two-seater featured a Ferrari-sourced V6 behind the driver, who was reclined almost prostrate beneath a wraparound windscreen.

Victory came quickly, with the Stratos winning the championship for three straight years until 1976 when Fiat allocated race funding to its far more boring 131 saloon.

Despite famously shoddy quality, particularly in the road-going versions that had to be built to meet homologation requirements, the Stratos instantly achieved a cult status that has never waned. Today a good one will set you back £250,000 and break down the second you touch it.

1973 **AC 3000ME** ▾

True to the form of many GT manufacturers of the period, AC decided to abandon the beautiful Frua-bodied 428 in favour of something suitably 70s: a mid-engined wedge. The 3000ME was a fibre-glass two-seater powered by a transverse Ford 3.0-litre V6 that sent power to the rear via an infamously problematic, in-house, five-speed gearbox. Although slightly dicey at the limit, the 3000 was a fine little machine that could put the wind up Porsche 911s of its era. Unfortunately, its production was hampered by the usual cash-flow chaos that blighted Britain's cottage car industry and its failure to pass basic crash testing.

In fact, it would be a full seven years before AC managed to get the car into proper production, by which time it was looking a little long in the tooth against the likes of the Lotus Esprit and Porsche 924.

1973 **BMW 2002 Turbo** ▸

BMW cemented its global reputation with the 2002. A successful works racing campaign gave it the credibility it needed as a practical yet highly advanced road car, but the cherry on the cake appeared in 1973 in the shape of a whopping great turbo.

This was the final evolution of the pre-3 Series Beemer, with bolt-on wheel arches and huge chin spoiler asserting brutal touring car menace. It was a ferocious thing to drive, too, with terrible turbo lag putting many 2002 Turbos and their unwitting drivers to the sword.

And if they weren't crashed they rusted, so finding a straight one today is nigh on impossible. Production lasted for a solitary year.

1973 **Matra-Simca Bagheera** ▶

Matra's rather inconsequential impression on French motoring history is not for lack of trying. After the weird-looking M530, the Bagheera was hailed as a deft example of form aligned with function. Here was a compact, sporty and fairly practical two-seater with a frugal engine, mid-mounted for superior weight distribution beneath a lightweight and undeniably pretty fastback, fibreglass body.

Unfortunately, Matra didn't do a thing to rustproof its steel chassis either, forcing the majority of Bagheeras into exceedingly early retirement.

1973 **Caterham Seven** ▼

With Lotus graduating to the big league by the late 60s, its much-admired but staggeringly basic Seven was no longer a serious business concern. In stepped Graham Nearn and Caterham Cars, buying up the rights to one of the simplest and most thrilling car designs of all time. Subtly evolving for the next 40 years, the Seven was and still is one of the clearest examples of Colin Chapman's genius.

1973 **Simca 1000 Rallye 2** ▶

Simca is an underreported entity outside of France where it made and sold huge numbers of cheap but highly regarded cars. The 1000 saloon was one of its stalwarts, built from 1961 until 1978, and the greatest evolution of this boxy, rear-engine, rear-drive four-door was the Rallye 2.

Simca used the most basic version of 'Le Mille' for its Rallye editions, providing invaluable lightness and freeing up funds for performance fettling. Lowered onto firmer suspension, fitted with disc brakes all round and now with improved cooling for the uprated 81bhp 1.3-litre engine, the Rallye 2 was agile and involving, if still a very long way from fast.

Finished in trademark bogey yellow with a matt-black bonnet and supplied with three standard seats and a racing bucket for the driver, the Rallye 2 became a pin-up for a generation of daydreaming French schoolboys.

1973 **Porsche 911 2.7 Carrera RS** ▼

The lightweight, race-tuned Carrera RS is the 911 all serious Porsche bores will be dreaming of when their eyes glaze over mid-conversation. And quite right, too. This was a milestone car for Porsche, evolving the near-perfect 911S in ways that wouldn't have appeared possible a few years before.

An even larger, flat-six engine meant more power, just about reined in by comprehensively uprated suspension, a wider rear track and the trademark rear ducktail spoiler.

Two versions were offered, Touring and Sport, the latter shaving a massive 100kg off the kerbweight with its thinner steel body and lightened glass.

Although strictly a homologation job, and therefore only requiring 500 road cars to be built for Porsche to take it racing, the factory more than tripled the necessary output – meaning an original RS is easy enough to find today, if not quite so easy to afford.

1973 **Lamborghini Urraco** ▶

With the oil crisis looming, there was something rather prescient about the Lamborghini Urraco, in that it was designed to be a more affordable alternative to the established hand-built, Italian, mid-engined supercars. Like the Ferrari 308 GT4 and Maserati Merak, the Urraco had a small displacement V8, providing more modest performance than the norm and, theoretically, a reduced ticket price. But it was still, when all was said and done, a hand-built, Italian, mid-engined supercar, and cost a massive £10,000 – more than the faster Ferrari – while returning a fairly lousy 18mpg.

1973 **Triumph Dolomite Sprint** ▼

A sprinkling of sporting fairy dust on the solid but worthy Triumph Dolomite produced one British Leyland's unsung greats, the Sprint. A tuned-up, 2.0-litre engine, combined with a lower ride, twin-exhaust and various subtle but distinctive styling cues, turned this ordinary three-box commuter into a proper little Q car. It was surprisingly rapid through the gears and topped out at nearly 120mph, an essential facet of the family four-door for all those balding, budding James Hunts. Modest rallying success soon followed until the faster TR7 tore past.

4 November 1973

In response to the global oil shortage the Netherlands organises 'car-free Sunday', during which the country's roads are deserted save for cyclists.

1973 **BMW 3.0 CSL** ▶

Another homologation special, this time built by BMW to compete in the European Touring Car Championship. In a similar vein to the legendary 911 2.7 Carrera RS, BMW's 3.0 CSL used thinner steel and aluminium to significantly reduce weight wherever possible, did away with sound-proofing and even used Perspex instead of glass in the side windows.
The most memorable features of the CSL, however, were its vast tail fins and rear spoiler, supplied unfitted to conform to Germany's strict road legislation. These earned it the apposite nickname 'the Batmobile'.

1973 **MGB GT V8** ▼

By the mid-70s, even the most die-hard patriot had grown tired of MG's slow and largely characterless B Roadster and fixed-head GT. Rover's lightweight 3.5-litre V8 offered a glimmer of hope, however, and for three years a small number of GTs were fitted with the dependable and highly tuneable lump.

Although still not devastatingly quick, the MGB GT now had bags of torque to exploit, and all without significant compromise to its handling.
Of over half a million MG Bs built, only around 2,500 were factory finished V8s, making these scarce and highly collectible variants of Britain's most ubiquitous and un-sporty sports car.

1973 **Bitter CD** ▼

Little known outside its native Germany, the Bitter CD was an elegant grand tourer in the old-school Italian mould, but built on sturdy modern underpinnings from Opel. Taken from an original design by Pietro Frua, the CD, for Coupé Diplomat, was built by the accomplished low-volume coachworks Baur and powered by a Chevrolet V8 from parent-company GM. The Bitter was beautifully made and beautiful to behold, but, like so many low-volume cars of the era, its potential was clobbered by the oil crisis. Production continued until 1979, but in tragically miniscule numbers.

1974 **Volkswagen Scirocco** ▶

Although built on the Golf platform, the first Scirocco was intended as a sportier alternative, with various performance revisions made to the chassis and suspension. Its attractive but understated fastback profile was the work of no less a designer than Giorgetto Giugiaro, who had penned the Lotus Esprit concept just a year before.

The Scirocco was a superbly made and wholly practical family hatchback blessed with Italian style and subtle performance tweaks, but it was to be comprehensively and perhaps unfairly outshone by the Mk1 Golf GTi that appeared just a year later.

1974 **Volvo 240 Estate** ▶

Over the years, Volvo had earned a reputation for building sensible, reliable, safety-first cars, a bedrock for the firm's future and the very essence of 1974's 200 Series. The mainstay 240 estate was a brick of a thing, slab-sided and tank like, with every safety advance available, including early but effective crumple zones.

This was the stuff of a million school runs and epic family road trips for multiple generations on multiple continents. So popular was the 240 that it stayed in production alongside its own replacement, only finally being phased out in Europe in 1993.

1974 **Vauxhall Firenza Baby Bertha** ▶

Itself a humble manufacturer of sensible, affordable fare, and using an unlovable coupé as its starting point, Vauxhall somehow managed to create one of the true legends of British motorsport.

Using parts from the Big Bertha racer, a promotional project that had snuffed it in the face of the '73 oil crisis, 'Baby Bertha' threw out the Firenza's stock 4-cylinder engine and replaced it with a 5.0-litre V8 from Aussie sister company Holden. With that came complex, race-honed suspension and running gear, and the legendary Gerry Marshall at the wheel.

Marshall and Baby Bertha won the Super Saloon series two years on the trot, creating the most iconic and admired car ever to have worn a Vauxhall badge.

14 September 1974
Jaguar ceases production of its iconic E-Type, having produced over 70,000 cars since 1961.

1974 **Lamborghini Countach LP400** ▼

Commissioned to replace the timelessly beautiful but ageing Miura, the Lamborghini Countach faced an unenviable task. Another stunning, mid-engined, V12 supercar was required quick-sharp – better to look at, better to drive.

It seems Marcello Gandini at Bertone was up to the challenge, however, creating one of the great shapes of the seventies. The LP400, with its sharp angles and scissor doors, was soon enshrined in every schoolboy's memory,

or at least stuck above their beds alongside vacant-looking women in heels and bikinis.

The Countach was a glorious dog. Terribly cramped, hot, noisy and impossible to see out of, it was indeed devastatingly quick, but also likely to spit you off the road without much in the way of provocation. Its 375bhp was good for nearly 200mph, but you'd have passed out with pure fear long before you got there.

1975 Volkswagen Golf GTi

When Volkswagen first roughed out its plan for a Beetle replacement, nothing would've got the design team fired faster than the suggestion of a high-performance variant. This was meant to be economical, practical family transport. Nothing more.

The GTi was a special project, undertaken in downtime by a group of engineers who recognised the potential of the supremely well-sorted, front-wheel-drive chassis and strong Audi-sourced engine.

With a few subtle modifications, including larger valves, higher compression and fuel injection in place of a carburettor, the Golf's 1600cc unit was tweaked up to 108bhp. Suddenly Wolfsburg's Johnny Sensible three-door hatchback could hit 60mph in under 10 seconds – an unprecedented figure in this segment – and wouldn't run out of puff until 110mph.

To the eternal credit of the top brass at VW, the car was championed from the outset, and artfully finished with lovely design details like the trademark red-grille surround and tartan sports seats. There was no looking back, with the GTi an immediate classic that altered the very fabric of the performance car market. This was a practical, reliable and broadly-speaking affordable hatchback that looked the business and, in real-world driving conditions, could do pretty much everything a period Porsche 911 could do for almost half the price and without trying to kill you on every wet roundabout.

Golf GTI Mk I

1975 **Porsche 911 Turbo** ▶

In the early 70s the Porsche 911 was a quick car with infamously tricky handling. Arguably the one thing it didn't need was a turbocharger. But in fitting one, Porsche created an icon so accomplished that it would barely evolve for the next 15 years.

In that time, it earned a deserved reputation as one the great sports cars, but also as something of a widow-maker. Many an exuberant yuppie fell foul of the 930's vicious turbo lag and tendency towards snap oversteer. Driven right, nothing could match it, but take liberties and you'd be going home in a bin bag.

1975 **Lancia Beta Montecarlo** ▼

Lancia's steady post-war decline was occasionally alleviated by a touch of the old magic. So it was with the Beta Montecarlo, a rakish, mid-engine, two-seat coupé. Despite the moneybags moniker the Montecarlo was an accessible offering, with little in the way of performance, or quality, to drive up the price. But it looked the business then and still does today. When it isn't riddled with rust.

1976 Rover SD1 ▶

There were never going to be many Rovers in a rundown of the coolest cars of all time, but the SD1 was a shoo-in. Conceived as a luxurious, attractive and economical executive saloon, the SD1 mated Rover's now legendary V8 to a three-speed automatic gearbox, combining performance and comfort with an undeniable kerbside presence, having shamelessly lifted design details from the Ferrari Daytona. A big hit with the police, white SD1s with that familiar orange stripe were rounding up wrong 'uns right through the 80s and carting them to the nick in rare style.

1976 Ferrari 512 BB ▼

The 512 Berlinetta Boxer replaced the front-engined Daytona, allowing Ferrari to offer a mid-engined V12 to rival the increasing might of Lamborghini. Capable of hitting 60mph in under six seconds and passing 170mph, this was a car that went like it looked like it should.

30 April 1975

Posters of bright red Ford Gran Torinos adorn the walls of adolescent boys' bedrooms for the next four years as Starsky and Hutch make their TV debut.

1976 **Bristol 603** ▶

Doubtless striking despair into the progress-o-phobic hearts of retired colonels and cigar-chewing captains of bygone industry, Bristol unveiled the 603 in 1976, a marginally more contemporary take on the luxurious 404 GT that had gone largely untroubled by the march of time for the last two decades. The 603 was, however, a huge success by Bristol's standards, so beloved by its exclusive, reclusive clientele that it also scarcely changed at all during its time in production. Power still came from massive and thirsty Chrysler V8s mated to automatic gearboxes. Speed, comfort, refinement and luxury were all there in spades. The price was reliably jaw-dropping.

1976 **TVR Taimar** ▲

Trying desperately to improve upon the M-Series without spending money they didn't have, TVR produced the Taimar. This was the 3000M, with its beefy Ford V6 and sweatbox cockpit, but with an opening rear hatch to make it fractionally more practical.

This car, and the Turbo version that followed, are highly significant, however. They marked the last of the classic TVRs, with design and shape easily traceable to the early 60s Grantura, before the company started building its disastrous wedge-shaped Tasmin. Things would never be the same.

1976 **Lotus Esprit S1** ▶

Probably Giorgetto Giugiaro's most famous design and a shape that remains instantly recognisable around the world some 40 years after it first appeared, the Lotus Esprit is the definitive 70s wedge.

Introduced to replace the low-volume Europa with a more convincing rival to the likes of the Ferrari 308, the Esprit adhered to Colin Chapman's low-weight philosophy with a steel backbone chassis and fibreglass body.

The original cars were powered by a modest 2.0-litre, Lotus-tuned engine, but any shortfall in poke was more than made up for by exceptional balance and handling.

1976 **Tyrell P34** ▼

Surely the weirdest car to ever win a Grand Prix, Ken Tyrrell's P34 was greeted with shock and mirth when it was revealed for the 1976 Formula 1 season. Its six-wheel design was not, however, without a certain brilliant logic, as having four smaller front tyres increased the amount of rubber in contact with the tarmac while improving front-end downforce. This didn't detract from the fact that the P34 looked very silly, and although it was consistently competitive in its first season, even posting a one-two win in Sweden, peculiar development demands saw it lose its edge by 1977.

1977 **Lada Niva** ▶

The laughing stock of the Cold War playground, Lada was and still is an honest and inexpensive Russian brand that makes surprisingly sturdy cars. Sturdiest amongst them was the Niva, a no-nonsense compact SUV that appeared in 1977 and remains in near-identical production today.

The Niva was designed to withstand the worst that a Russian winter could throw at it, which is really quite a lot, while still being cheap to build, buy and maintain. With permanent four-wheel drive, front, central and rear diffs and a low ratio box, this was a formidable off-road machine for European hatchback money.

1977 **Matra-Simca Rancho** ▶

In what could be argued was a moment of perfect insanity, low-volume French sporsts car manufacturer Matra spied an improbable gap in the market to build a cheap pseudo-offroad vehicle for European swanks who wanted a slice of the landed lifestyle on a shoestring. Thirty years on, this has become almost universal practise, but back then Matra was ploughing a fairly lonely furrow.

The Rancho, built in conjunction with new partner Simca, was a fibreglass-bodied hotchpotch of bits from Simca saloons, including its weedy petrol engine and rudimentary front-wheel drive. But it had a bonkers Gallic charm which, when coupled with its undeniable practicality, kept customers coming into the mid-80s.

◀ 1977 **Aston Martin V8 Vantage**

What the original V8 Aston sorely lacked was proper poke, a shortcoming ably redressed by the Vantage. This performance and aerodynamic rethink fettled the 5.3-litre V8 to a high state of tune, creating one of the fastest-accelerating production cars of the period: 60mph was seen off in just 5.3 seconds, with a possible top speed of 170mph.

It still didn't go round corners terribly convincingly, however, and many Vantages were hastily retro-fitted with a sports-handling pack to keep them on the straight and narrow.

This was the Formula 1 car that ushered in the era of turbocharging. Using a tiny, 1.5-litre, six-cylinder engine when the rest of the paddock were still on 3.0-litre flat-12s, the RS01 paved the way for one of F1's wildest periods, with cars in qualifying trim exceeding 1400bhp, all of it fed through manual gearboxes with no such luxuries as traction control.

Renault's daring turbo debutante took two years to become remotely competitive, but ultimately won an impressive 15 Grand Prix. By the time the rest of the teams had cottoned on, Renault had abandoned F1, but its parting shot had been a great one.

1977 **Lotus 78 JPS** ▼

So very 70s in its black-and-gold John Player Special livery, the Lotus 78 was yet another milestone in Colin Chapman's peerless engineering career. The 78 became known as the 'ground-effect car' after wind-tunnel testing created an ingenious means of accelerating air under the car to suck it to the road. Although not as successful as it might have been, the 78 marked another huge turning point in F1's approach to aerodynamics.

1977 Saab 99 Turbo ▼

Appearing in the salad days of forced induction, the Saab 99 Turbo was the first sensible car to benefit from a blower. This was a safe, practical family hatch that was suddenly available in Warp Speed trim. With an eight-second 0–60mph time and even more impressive in-gear grunt, the 99 Turbo was indecently quick for the late 70s and is no slouch even now.

Saab's motives in producing the 99 Turbo were typically sound however: turbocharging was the best way to cope with stringent emissions regulations in the key US market. But the upshot was an instant performance classic that would influence automotive engineering for years to come.

1978 Subaru MV1800 ▶

Although Subaru is inextricably linked to the Impreza after its WRC dominance, the four-wheel drive technology that garnered all the silverware once had earthier applications. The MV1800, also known as the Brat, was a hard-graft pick-up that shared styling with the Chevy El Camino.
Incredibly rare now, thanks to the fatal combination of 70s Japanese rust awareness and off-road ability, the MV1800 is becoming an unlikely collectors' item.

1978 **Brabham BT46** ▼

A direct response to the Lotus 78's ground effect, Brabham's BT46b 'fan car' was the offspring of another British racing genius, Gordon Murray. Purportedly for cooling the car's hot and heavy Alfa Romeo flat-12, the gigantic rear-mounted fan was actually designed to suck air from under the car to increase downforce. Brilliantly effective but not strictly speaking legal, it was banned by the FIA after just one race, which it had won with consummate ease.

1978 **Mazda RX-7** ▶

Almost as far ahead of its time on the outside as it was within, the RX-7 launched Mazda and its Wankel rotary engine onto the international sports car stage. The Wankel's compact dimensions and low weight enabled the RX-7 to be beautifully balanced, but it was a thirsty bugger with enough maintenance issues to keep the sceptics very sceptical.

1978 **BMW M1**

An invaluable ingredient for road-going kudos is racing pedigree. It's what made so many of the dual-purpose sports cars of the 60s truly great, and what ensures more modern homologation specials have an edge of desirability over purely street-oriented fare.

The BMW M1 was designed to go racing in the Group 4 World Championship, but due to various delays and rule changes ended up competing in its own single-make series. These hugely powerful M1 Procars were raced as a preamble to the Formula 1 Grand Prix, often driven by the F1 elite, which created a groundswell of interest.

The first 'M' car, the M1 remains BMW's only production mid-engined, road-goer, using a bespoke 3.5-litre straight-six that went on to power the original M5. Initially a joint project with Lamborghini, the M1's fibreglass bodywork was penned by Giugiaro, and its blend of German engineering with Italian supercar styling made it one of the finest-looking and most sought-after machines of its day.

Inside the M1, despite being pared back for lightness and devoid of the more obvious frills of big-money exotica, the cabin was extremely comfortable and refined. Although somewhat detuned from the 800+bhp available in the Procar, performance was up there with the very best of the period. Sixty was yours in under six seconds with a top speed of over 160mph.

Ultra-rare and decidedly pricey, the M1 became a legend in its own lifetime as a real road car with racing genes, rather than a racing car with a radio.

1979 **Talbot Sunbeam Lotus** ▶

The Talbot Sunbeam Lotus was a typically plucky British underdog. Built on a shoestring thanks to a shortage of both funding and sponsorship, the modest Sunbeam three-door hatch was fettled by Lotus's race engineers to take part in the World Rally Championship. The massive, and massively wealthy, teams from Audi, Ford and Opel could only watch and weep as the Talbot began racking up class and overall wins around the world, finally taking the title in 1981.

1979 **Mercedes-Benz G-Wagen** ▼

The Gelandewagen is Germany's answer to the Land Rover, an incredibly tough off-road vehicle with both military and civilian applications. But the thing that sets the G-Wagen apart from its long-running British alternative is, in a word, quality. While a brand new Land Rover Defender is leaching pints of engine oil on to the showroom floor, the G looks after itself for years with only basic maintenance. Ruinously expensive new, and still an affront to the frugal in 30-year-old rust-bucket spec, the G-Wagen is a top-shelf fantasy for the working man, finding most of its modern-day custom in bling-hungry media and mafia.

1979 **Oldsmobile Nascar** ▼

In a vintage year of NASCAR featuring the grizzly blue-collar talents of veteran Richard Petty and rookie Dale Earnhardt, fans witnessed mid-race punch-ups and unprecedented top speeds. Petty won the blue-riband Daytona 500 in his STP Oldsmobile Cutlass after title rivals Cale Yarborough and Donnie Allinson crashed out together. These men then became embroiled in a bloody trackside brawl, all captured for the nation on live TV. Formula 1 this was not. Petty and his iconic number 43 Cutlass went on to win the championship, his last of a remarkable and record-breaking seven.

4 May 1979

Margaret Thatcher becomes the western world's first woman Prime Minister and chooses a suitably British mode of transport, arriving at the door of 10 Downing Street in a Rover P5B, of which Queen Elizabeth II is also reportedly a fan.

1980s SPANDEX AND TURBOCHARGERS

The 80s was not a rosy period for Britain's once-great manufacturing industry. 'Homegrown' began capitulating to the superior economic model of 'getting Johnny Foreigner to do it for half the money'. A good time to be a fat cat maybe, but not so much for the minions on the empty factory floors.

This was the era of greed and guilt, of red-faced yuppies in red braces driving red Porsches and a spittle-flecked Bob Geldof trying to get the rest of us to feed a starving African subcontinent.

The best we had to offer in terms of cars were shadows of former selves from the likes of Aston and Lotus, and our mass-production dross was hitting new lows of ennui-inducing averageness.

On a socio-political level things were better. Britain took a final hit of its empire-building elixir by booting the Argentines off the Falkland Islands while a leathery redneck in the Whitehouse somehow oversaw the dismantling of the Iron Curtain. For the first time in ages it looked like we weren't all going to expire cowering beneath mattresses under the stairs.

Closer to home things were strangely polarised, especially for our nation's disaffected youth. Music went synth, with everything mimed over banks of Casio keyboards by New Romantics in heavy blusher. It was either that or punk, which involved getting very spotty and sticking pins through your cheeks.

If you were rich you stayed at home all day for the first time in history, playing Nintendo, watching Dire Straits on MTV and backcombing. If you were poor you went out and spray-painted novel obscenities onto an Austin Montego.

Strange times, but a period of rapid technological progress that gave birth to some motoring magic. The red-raw Ferrari F40 went head-to-head with Porsche's space-aged 959 in the ultimate supercar showdown, and maniacal Group B rally arrived and as quickly departed, watched through trembling fingers. The decade of excess, of haves and have-nots, the 80s was a brilliant catastrophe. At least they finally stopped building the MGB.

1980 Mercedes-Benz 500 SEC ▶

Costing considerably more than the average house and taking up about as much space, the luxurious, innovative, fast and thirsty 500 SEC was the ultimate 80s coupé. Mercedes-Benz could scarcely have chosen a better time in which to peddle this celebration of unnecessary wealth. Powered by a 5.0-litre V8 and featuring novel luxuries like fully adjustable powered and heated seats, this was the definition of extravagance for the easy-money generation.

1980 Audi Quattro ▼

The first car to feature Audi's game-shifting four-wheel-drive system, the Quattro was a turbocharged coupé based on the humble Audi 80 saloon. The blown, in-line, five-cylinder engine and extraordinary levels of grip made the Quattro a devastatingly quick machine in even comparatively novice hands.

No mass-production car had offered the safety and performance attributes of four-wheel drive before, let alone while mated to a turbocharger. The Quattro changed everything for Audi and sent rival designers back to the drawing board around the world.

1980 **Aston Martin Bulldog** ▶

The mid-engined supercar market is a place where few Britons dare to tread, although Aston's first brief foray makes you wonder why. The Bulldog had all the right ingredients to stick it to Ferrari and Lamborghini: namely a 43-inch roofline, gull-wing doors and a claimed top speed way in excess of 200mph. Sadly, the proposed production of 25 cars never made it beyond the original concept before Aston's financial shitstorm caused the plug to be pulled.

1980 **Renault 5 Turbo** ▼

One of the first road cars to appear as a direct result of the lunatic Group 4 rally series, the R5 Turbo was a limited homologation run of Renault 5s with a turbocharged engine mounted where the rear seats used to be. A white-knuckle drive thanks to its lag-heavy turbo and short wheelbase, the R5 was better suited to the competitions it had been conceived for, winning the Monte Carlo rally on its debut.

1980 **Matra Murena** ▲

An under-appreciated effort from the tiny French outfit, the Matra Murena redressed the rust problems suffered by the Bagheera by galvanising its chassis. Still light and finely balanced thanks to its fibreglass construction and mid-engined layout, the Murena was an affordable and capable little sports car with bold styling both inside and out. Sadly production was halted after just three years when Matra began building the ground-breaking but thunderously uncool Renault Espace instead.

1980 **Alfa Romeo GTV6** ▶

Another artful offering from the prolific Giorgetto Giugiaro, Alfa Romeo's boxy Alfetta saloon was brilliantly reborn as the rakish fastback GTV coupé. Praised for its looks and handling, the one thing the GTV lacked was a proper engine.

Six years after production started, Alfa finally addressed the problem by creating a bonnet bulge under which it wedged the 2.5 V6 from its luxury '6' saloon. With reliable and efficient Bosch fuel injection also installed, the marriage was perfectly consummated. The GTV6 became a dominant force on the European touring car circuit and remains a cult classic around the world. The 80s is not a memorable decade for even the most ardent Alfa enthusiast, but the GTV6 provides the perfect pair of rose-tinted spectacles.

1981 **Opel Ascona 400** ▶

In the late 70s, Opel began to develop a rally car based on its budget Ascona saloon. But being a German company with strong British affiliation through Vauxhall meant the net could be cast unusually wide in the talent pool. Using the combined might of homegrown designers Irmscher and Tommy tuners Cosworth, the Ascona 400 burst onto the WRC in 1982, winning the driver's championship in the hands of rally god Walter Rohrl. And this was to be the last rear-wheel drive car to do so.

1981 **Lamborghini Jalpa** ▼

Sold alongside the flagship Countach as a more accessible entry point to Lamborghini ownership, the odd-looking Jalpa has become little more than a footnote in the marque's illustrious history. Using a 3.5-litre V8 instead of the customary V12, the mid-engined Jalpa was indeed markedly cheaper than its big brother and a deal easier to get on with. Although production was typically tiny, this was still one of the best-selling Lambos of the pre-Audi era and the only one to have used eight cylinders where twelve would do.

8 October 1980

Grannies the world over rejoice as the Mini Metro meanders on to the motoring scene.

1982 **Renault 5 Gordini Turbo** ▶

With the Group 4 R5 Turbo swelling an already gonflé Gallic pride in its homegrown rallying record, the market was ripe for a blown version of the warmed-up Renault 5 Alpine. Known as the Gordini Turbo in the UK where Sunbeam owned the 'Alpine' name, the new car featured different wheels and both uprated gearbox and brakes to cope with the extra power and punchy delivery from its single Garrett turbocharger.

Sadly, the Gordini became a rite of passage for boy-racers, meaning that most right-hand drive examples have been ruined by aftermarket add-ons, neglect or enormous accidents. Often all three.

1982 **Mitsubishi Starion** ▼

Apace with Japan's surge into the sports car market, Mitsubishi unveiled the bizarrely named Starion. This followed the usual format of front-engine, rear-wheel drive and a token rear row of seats, but its USP was a turbocharger.

With 168bhp now on tap, the Starion could see off 60mph in 8.3 seconds and ran out of puff at over 130mph, making it more than a match for European rivals like the Porsche 924. Best had in later, inter-cooled wide-body form, the Starion is now an unloved bargain: the archetypal future classic.

1982 **Porsche 956** ▼

Designed to take part in the newly formed Group C sports car championship, the 956 would quickly become its dominant force and one of Porsche's most successful racing cars. Driven by Brit Derek Bell and his team-mate Jacky Ickx, the 956 led from the start at Le Mans in its inaugural year, winning ahead of two more identical factory cars.

Featuring design firsts like a dual clutch and aluminium monocoque, the 956 was typically ingenious, expensive and untouchable on track.

Tragedy haunted this car, however, with up-and-coming F1 ace Stefan Bellof dying in his privateer 956 at Spa in an incident with Ickx. The car lost popularity soon after and was gone from competition by the end of 1986.

After a long sojourn from the international sports car circuit, Aston martin attempted a comeback of sorts with a hotchpotch Group C racer. The car was developed by Nimrod Racing on a Lola-designed chassis, with Aston's only discernible input beyond financial backing being a strengthened version of its 5.4-litre V8 engine. The idea was that the Nimrod would be a useful publicity tool for Aston, whose new co-owner, Victor Gauntlet, was an amateur racing nut. Unfortunately, the car wasn't terribly competitive against the likes of Porsche's unassailable 956, its best outing being a seventh place at Le Mans in 1982. It was, nevertheless, stirring stuff to see Aston Martin back in the big league of endurance racing, all the more so in hindsight: it would be another 25 years before the marque returned to Le Mans.

I January 1982

The new Datsun 280ZX Turbo is announced for the American market, complete with futuristic talking dashboard. Nine months later, Knightrider appears on TV screens, immediately making Datsun's gimmicky marketing toy the single coolest thing on the planet.

1982 **Lancia 037** ▼

Built specifically for the new and now infamous Group B, the Lancia 037 exploded onto the international rally scene by taking the debut manufacturer's title in a shower of gravel and snow. Sideways for most of the year, it was the only car to win with rear-wheel drive before the Audi Quattro permanently shifted the goal posts. The 037 is instantly familiar to a generation of rally fans, partly down to that unique and aggressive profile – distantly based on the Beta Montecarlo – and partly thanks to its glorious Martini livery.

With its small, but heavily supercharged, 2.0-litre engine, the 037 was immensely fast, at times too much for the tight and unpredictable routes and surfaces of the WRC. Along with its Delta S4 successor, the 037 was involved in the two fatal accidents that ultimately led to the demise of Group B.

1983 GMC Vandura ▶

Although it goes without saying that ungainly American vans from the early 80s are not, in the strictest contextual sense, cool, an exception has to be made for the GMC Vandura. For anyone growing up in the era of the trashy US adventure series, the Vandura is rightly only ever referred to as 'The A-Team Van'.

With its go-faster stripe, roof spoiler and sliding door out of which would tumble history's only crack team of non-lethal mercenaries, this rear-wheel drive, V8-powered lump of artless functionality has a very special place in every schoolboy's heart.

◀ 1983 Fiat Panda 4x4

Always beloved of Northern Italy's Alpine police and today regarded as something of a collector's item, the Fiat Panda 4x4 was a breakthrough piece of engineering back in 1983. Easily the smallest car on sale that offered four-wheel drive, the Panda's manually selectable off-road system was designed and built by Steyr-Puch, the Austrian team behind the Mercedes-Benz G-Wagen. Its matchless combination of low weight and grip gave it unbelievable off-road abilities.

1983 Mercedes-Benz 190E 2.3-16 Cosworth ▶

Created to allow Mercedes-Benz to take part in the DTM touring car championship, the homologated 2.3-16 mated the legendary build quality of Merc's 190 with the proven performance tuning of Cosworth. The 2.3-litre, 16-valve engine was good for 143mph, the driving experience one of total Germanic assurance. With its subtle styling, poise and potency, this was the thinking man's M3 before the M3 had even been invented.

1984 **Subaru Justy** ▶

Before it recently reappeared as a rebranded Daihatsu, Subaru's Justy was a stout and functional three- (or five-) door hatch that was offered with a secret weapon: permanent four-wheel drive. Hen's teeth rare now thanks to the rust that plagues so many Japanese exports from the 80s, the original Justy is highly prized in any condition as a pocket rally pretender or the ultimate rural runabout.

1984 **Skoda Estelle** ▼

Pre-VW-era Skodas were the source of some derision on the roads of Western Europe, but the solid, simple Estelle had a trick up its Eastern Bloc sleeve. The worthy little four-door saloon had a rear-engined, rear-wheel-drive configuration that helped turn it into a rallying record-breaker.

Despite significant budget limitations, the stout and surprisingly dependable Estelle racked up numerous class wins throughout the Group B era, particularly on Britain's RAC rally where it was a competitive presence for half a decade.

1984 **Ferrari 288 GTO** ▾

Another supercar born out of an unfulfilled desire to go racing, the 288 GTO was crafted as Ferrari's entrant to the Group B GT series, an event that never even started due to a lack of interest from other manufacturers, so every one of nearly 300 race-ready supercars went straight onto the public road.

Loosely based on the 308 GTB, the 288 GTO featured an enlarged and twin-turbocharged engine, wider track and lighter body. It was, needless to say, terrifyingly quick for road use, with a 0–60mph time of around 4 seconds and a top speed nudging 190mph.

1984 **Ferrari Testarossa** ▶

While the 288 GTO was being developed with a raw, racing focus, Ferrari had also been at work on its latest, most civilised road car. The Testarossa is for many the quintessential 80s supercar, with its trademark slatted side pods feeding air to the 4.9-litre flat-12 mounted just behind the driver.
The Testarossa offered the consummate balance of performance and luxury for the period, and marked a turning point in Ferrari's evolution. This car, along with the later TR and M variants, would be the last high-volume, mid-engined V12 to exit the gates at Maranello.

◀ 1984 **MG Metro 6R4**

For most people, Group B evokes images of Quattro Sports and Lancia Deltas – exotic, desirable homologation specials with formidable road-going siblings. But a certain cross-section of British rally aficionados think only of the Austin Metro.
In 1984, this hateful granny wagon was taken to the highest level of international rallying, having been rebuilt with a 400bhp, 3.0-litre V6 mounted amidships beneath a be-winged and lightweight body.
Reliability issues prevented the immediately competitive four-wheel drive 6R4 from ever finding its feet before Group B was banned, thus denying the humble Austin its ticket to certain classic status.

◀ 1984 **Peugeot 205 GTI**

While the willy-waving Italian and German supercar space race continued unabashed, in a quiet corner of France, the frequently forgettable Peugeot was putting together one of the great driver's cars of all time.
Based on its future-proof but unexciting three-door family hatchback, the 205 GTi was immediately recognised as one of the best front-wheel drive performance cars the world had seen.
Even today its impact is still felt, with modern hot-hatches lacking the immediacy and involvement of the tricky but rewarding 205. A legend was born here, one that Peugeot has sadly never managed to match.

21 October 1984

Niki Lauda snatches victory from Alain Prost by just half a point to clinch the Formula 1 world championship crown in the closest season in the history of the sport.

1984 **Porsche 911 4x4 Paris-Dakar** ▼

Not content with demolishing all comers on the international sports car circuit, Porsche set about winning 'the toughest race on earth' with its seemingly impregnable 911. The Paris-Dakar prepared '953', used developmental elements of the as-yet-unseen 959 supercar, including its immensely advanced four-wheel drive system with ground-breaking torque vectoring technology. The Rothmans liveried Porsche won it at the first attempt – no mean feat on a 5,000-mile hack through the African desert – but was rendered obsolete the following year by the rallying rendition of the 959.

1985 Peugeot 205 T16 ▶

Bearing a strong but illusory resemblance to the humble 205 hatchback, the T16 was actually a ground-up redesign for Peugeot to take part in the now well-established Group B rally.

Its turbocharged, 16-valve four-pot was plonked behind the driver, powering all four wheels beneath a flimsy and feather-light fibreglass body. With around 450bhp on tap and the heroic Finn Timo Salonen at the wheel, the T16 won the 1985 drivers' and constructors' championships. Peugeot would do the double again in '86, but by then Group B was in terminal decline thanks to a series of high-profile fatalities.

1985 Lancia Delta S4 ▼

Although an astonishingly fast and capable rally car, the Delta S4 will always be remembered as another nail in Group B's coffin. With its low weight, four-wheel drive and both turbo and supercharged power delivery, the S4 was a match for the Audi Quattros, but showed fewer concessions to driver safety. With fuel tanks beneath the driver and rumours – that are still only rumours – that Lancia was concealing highly-flammable nitrous oxide in the roll cage to give an extra performance boost, the S4 was a firework looking for a spark. And the spark came when driver Henri Toivonen and his co-driver Sergio Cresto left a stage at speed on the '86 Corsican Rally and died in the ensuing fireball.

1985 **Audi Sport Quattro S1** ▼

Audi's 'Sport' Quattro was built to Group B specification, dramatically shortening the standard car's wheelbase to leave prominent overhangs and an oddly upright windscreen. The body was Kevlar-reinforced fibreglass, incredibly light and strong.

The final evolution of this game-changing world champion was the S1. Readied for the 1986 season, its turbocharged, in-line, five-cylinder engine was now equipped with an ingenious recycling system to keep it on boost even when the throttle was off. This meant that peak engine power – reputedly approaching 600bhp – was almost instantly available the moment the driver was back on the gas. The other, more obvious, change from the

year before was the aerodynamic package, which included a huge rear wing, gaping side pods for a rear-mounted radiator and prominent 'snowplough' chin spoiler. It looked ludicrous, in a very, very good way.

But Group B was dicing with the laws of physics, its cars simply too fast for the routes they were on and the drivers at the helm. An accident involving a Ford RS200 early in the season saw three spectators killed and over 30 injured, convincing Audi to pull the S1 from the WRC immediately despite immense investment and winning potential. The decision was as prescient as it was respectful, however, since further fatalities later in the year would cause the whole championship to be officially cancelled.

◄ 1985 **BMW M5**

Using a slightly detuned version of the now defunct M1 supercar's race-honed straight-six, BMW's Motorsport division cooked up the world's fastest saloon car in the M5. Its 282bhp was good for 60mph in six seconds and a top speed in excess of 150mph. This was ruggedly reliable, practical motoring with the performance of a contemporary Porsche 911. The supersaloon was born, the sportscar rulebook rewritten.

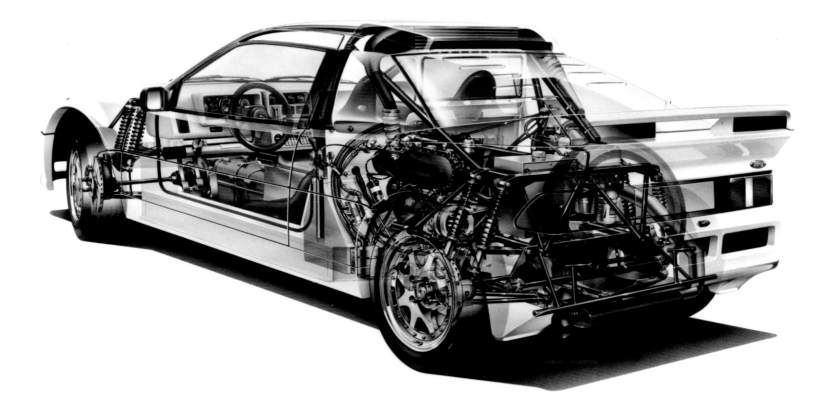

1986 **Ford RS200** ▲

Hastily prepared for WRC's Group B, the Ford RS200 was a purpose-built rally car with no real world relation beyond the 200 road-going versions built for homologation. Styled by Ghia, its mid-engined layout offered superb handling balance and excellent grip from its complex four-wheel drive system. But Ford never resolved the issue of turbo lag from its small capacity Cosworth-tuned engine, making the RS200 far more challenging to drive than its purposeful profile would suggest.

Although unveiled in 1984, Ford didn't finish the requisite 200 road cars until '86, the final season of Group B and a particularly disastrous competitive debut for the RS. One of the works cars was involved in an accident in Portugal that killed three spectators and injured countless more. The incident spelled the beginning of the end for the increasingly hazardous Group B, and Ford's monumental investment – rumoured to be in the region of £10 million – had apparently been squandered.

◄ 1986 **Porsche 944 Turbo**

Sold alongside the 924 it was effectively replacing, the 944 was a significant evolution of Porsche's front-engined sports car, with an enlarged 4-cylinder engine, wider track and greater refinement. Proper Porsche performance was still lacking, however, until the Turbo appeared four years into production. Near-perfect neutral handling, now backed up by a 0–60mph time of under six seconds and 150mph top speed, made this a seriously tempting alternative to the trickier, pricier 911.

1986 **Lancia Thema 8.32** ▶

Thanks to its formidable presence on the international rally scene and the offshoot success of its Delta HF hot-hatch, Lancia was back to being a sporting brand after a lengthy period in the performance doldrums. To capitalise on this, it jazzed up the boring four-door Thema saloon by stuffing the 3.0-litre V8 from the Ferrari 308 under the bonnet.

It was a detuned version, however, and assembled by Ducati because Ferrari was busy. To make matters worse, the standard Thema Turbo was quicker. Nevertheless, open the bonnet of your otherwise bollocks 80s three-box and there, on the rocker cover, was the word 'Ferrari'. Class.

1986 **Renault Alpine GTA** ▼

Developed by rally legends Alpine but sold in the UK by parent company Renault, the GTA was another logical and intriguing evolution of Alpine's fibreglass body and rear-engine philosophy. A bargain supercar for the 80s, the GTA and especially its later Turbo variant were a match for far pricier contemporaries like the Porsche 911, thanks to excellent traction and a low kerbweight.

Using radical polyester components helped make it very light, while Renault's less adventurous but mercifully uncomplicated Douvrin 2.8 V6 supplied characterful, plentiful power.

Nowadays the GTA is still a bargain, but scarcity means prices are creeping up on this future classic.

1986 **Ford Sierra RS Cosworth** ▼

At its peak popularity the Sierra RS Cosworth had the dubious honour of being the most commonly stolen car in Britain, a fact that, combined with its raw performance and blue-collar following, made it almost as expensive to insure as it was to buy.

With rear-wheel drive and a bespoke Cosworth engine good for 200bhp in standard road-going trim, the RS was a runaway success, with demand outstripping the limited supply of just 5,000 cars. Also a favoured getaway car, the RS Cossie is part of underworld folklore.

C235 HVW

12 February 1986

The British and French agree to dig a tunnel under the English Channel, but motorists can't just drive to France 45 metres below the sea bed – ventilation and safety issues mean vehicles are loaded onto trains for the journey.

1986 **BMW M3 E30** ▼

The original M3 is still regarded by BMW cognoscenti as the one to have. Born of Beemer's desire to race in Group A touring cars against the likes of the Mercedes-Benz 2.3-16, the road-going M3 was another homologation special, with just 500 units turned out to satisfy the regulators at the FIA. The M3 retained much of the racer's purity and focus, making it a demanding but ultimately highly-rewarding driver's car. A slightly ominous reputation for sudden and violent oversteer, coupled with its aggressive competition aero-kit and flared arches, made the E30 M3 the stuff of petrolhead folklore. Nowadays, however, a tidy example is yours for middleweight Ford Focus money.

1986 **Porsche 959** ▶

Conceived as a technological test-bed and sold in highly limited numbers for toe-curling money, the 959 is one of Porsche's rarest and most important road cars. Featuring a revolutionary, torque-vectoring, all-wheel drive system and bespoke, flat-six engine with sequential twin turbos, the 959 was way ahead of the mid-80s game, paving the way for all future 911s.

Originally destined for the stillborn Group B sportscar series, the 959 was built of aluminium and Kevlar to maximise rigidity and minimise weight. Performance, unsurprisingly, was simply staggering, with 60mph up in 3.6 seconds and a top speed of 197mph.

It cost £150,000 in road-going trim, though, a truly monumental amount of money back in 1986. Yet despite the gob-smacking list price, Porsche is rumoured to have lost as much again on every one it sold.

1986 **Lamborghini LM002** ▼

Looking remarkably similar to the original Humvee, Lamborghini's sole crack at the off-road market appeared at much the same time and was also intended for the US military. No uptake from Uncle Sam meant pedalling a few to desert-dwelling civilian punters to cover costs, and the LM002 established itself as a lifestyle statement in the oil-rich Middle East instead, which would prove ironic. Made of angular aluminium and fibreglass to keep the weight down, the V12 LM002 was the first Lambo to feature four-wheel drive and could hit 60mph in a remarkable 7.7 seconds.

1987 Lancia Delta Integrale ▼

With Lancia still a competitive force in the World Rally Championship, the road-going, front-wheel drive Delta HF was ripe for further exploitation. Evolved and advanced in every direction, the homologated Integrale 8v would become one of Lancia's greatest road cars and an 80s icon on a par with the Audi Quattro and BMW M3. A far bigger and smoother engine with enlarged turbocharging brought the Delta's power up to 185bhp, while the addition of four-wheel drive beneath aggressively flared arches gave it traction and presence to match. Although only sold in left-hand drive and with a problematic fondness for rust, the original Integrale is recognised as a true classic these days and a former bargain now commands increasingly stratospheric prices.

25 November 1987

Following the demise of the Group B category the previous year, Lancia dominate the Group A World Rally Championship in 1984, sealing victory for the season in emphatic style with a triumph at the final stage in Wales.

1987 Porsche RUF Yellowbird ▼

It's never long after a superb sports car has been launched that an aftermarket tuner steps forward and comprehensively ruins it. One of the more notable exceptions to the rule, however, is RUF, a small but highly regarded German outfit that has been fettling 911s since 1977. RUF went global 10 years later when they created the CTR, nicknamed the Yellowbird. This was a rebuilt version of the standard 3.2-litre Carrera, incorporating aluminium panels, fibreglass bumpers and an obsessive level of streamlining to minimise drag.

The engine was given a thorough going-over, too, of course, with increased capacity, high-performance injection and two massive turbochargers. The result was a frankly troubling 469bhp in a car that weighed a little over a tonne. Small wonder then that the CTR was quickly recognised at the fastest production road car in the world, with its astonishing top speed of 211mph. And it still had the handling characteristics of a mid-80s 911. Compelling, terrifying stuff.

1987 Alfa Romeo 75 3.0 V6 ▶

Awkwardly angular to behold these days and remembered for its less-than-perfect build quality, Alfa Romeo's 75 was, nevertheless, a highly desirable sporting saloon in its time. Blessed with near-perfect front-rear-weight distribution thanks to the unusual use of a transaxle in a road-going saloon, the rear-wheel drive 75 had proper sporting potential in a period where the average family four-door was becoming horrendously sensible.

The 3.0-litre V6 appeared in 1987, with a limited slip diff and 153bhp to play with. Alfa entered the Group A racing series at the same time, turning Giuseppe Public's daily commute into a whiteknuckle touring car fantasy.

1987 **Ferrari F40**

Life begins at 40, so it's said, and Ferrari chose to mark the date by making the most memorable and sought-after car in Maranello's modern epoch.

The F40 was based on the 288 GTO Group B car, but designed as a road-going special to be made in ultra-limited numbers for a select-few respected clients. Not for the last time, exclusivity would take a backseat to the bottom line when demand for the F40 went through the roof. Ferrari built around three times as many as originally planned, somewhat diluting the investment potential for those early takers.

Nevertheless, the F40 is now universally hankered for and worth as much as the next plutocrat is willing to spend when he sees Rosso Corsa at auction. And it's easy to see why. This was to be Enzo's swansong. Il Capo was in his nineties by now and determined to see Ferrari stick it to the rest of the world one last time. So power was up even from the monumentally quick 288 GTO, with the turbocharged V8 now making 478bhp. Couple that with its slick and timeless wind tunnel-tested composite body and the F40 was good for over 200mph, having passed 60mph in less than four seconds.

It cost £193,000, however, which, back in 1987, was like the national debt of a reasonably large African country – and for that you got a cabin with tissue-thin grey carpet, plastic windows, no air con, no stereo and bits of string instead of door handles. This was a committed driver's car, then, one that would test the skills of the helmsman and the patience of his passenger in equal measure. But it was also fitting testament to the uncompromising focus of the great man and the engineering brilliance he oversaw. The F40 is the definitive 80s supercar and remains the ultimate Ferrari of the V8 era.

1988 **Volkswagen Corrado** ▶

Following the same format as the Scirocco it replaced, Volkswagen's all-new Corrado coupé concealed sturdy Golf underpinnings beneath a subtle but attractive 2+2 fastback body.

Although still front-wheel drive, the Corrado was convincingly sporty, with assured and predictable handling. Power started with VW's solid 1.8-litre, 4-cylinder unit, in either 8 or sportier 16v guise, but the one to have was the supercharged G60.

This developed 158bhp, which was more than the equivalent Golf GTI and as much as any manufacturer cared to put through the steering wheels in those days. Good enough for a sub-nine-second dash to 60mph and a top speed of 137mph, the G60 provided a pricey but impressive performance alternative to the increasingly ubiquitous Mk II GTi.

◀ 1988 **Toyota Celica**

Toyota had slowly been establishing itself on the WRC, although rear-wheel drive and Group B power had proved a tricky combination. The Celica GT4 ST165 appeared for the inaugural 1988 Group A season, finally equipped with four-wheel drive and the immense driving talents of Carlos Sainz and Juha Kankkunen. Victories came thick and fast for both factory cars. In the right conditions, which were usually the wrong ones for all the other teams, the Celica seemed utterly at home.

◀ 1989 **Alfa Romeo SZ**

As divisive today as it was back then, Alfa Romeo's SZ quickly earned the nickname 'Il Mostro' – The Monster. Conceived as a joint project between Alfa Romeo, Fiat and coachbuilders Zagato, the SZ was a truly bonkers vision of late 80s design, formed from slabs of lightweight thermoplastic that were then bolted to the underpinnings of a V6 Alfa 75 saloon.

The looks will split opinion until the world stops turning, but legendary grip from its race-derived suspension and bellicose exhaust note unite the majority behind this improbably capable and intoxicating machine.

1988 **Jaguar XJR-9** ▼

Tasked with taking Jaguar back to the top of sports car racing after decades of inactivity, the XJR-9 was designed and built out-of-house by Tom Walkinshaw Racing, but with full factory support. This was a daunting time to be entering Group C, with Porsche's 962s dominating race after race, year after year. Walkinshaw and his team were unfazed, however. After two seasons of rapid development the Jaguar comfortably won the championship in 1987, although that vital Le Mans victory eluded them.

The stage was set for a blistering showdown in the following year, however, and Walkinshaw did not disappoint. With 720bhp on tap from its 7.0-litre V12, the 245mph Silk Cut liveried R-9 battled the Porches for a total race distance of over 3,300 miles, finishing ahead of the lead 962 by little over a minute. This was Porsche's first loss at Le Sarthe in eight years and, even more significantly, Jaguar's first win since the Ecurie Ecosse D-Types of 1957.

14 August 1988

Enzo Ferrari's pursuit of speed finally comes to an end, as he passes away aged 90. The Italian Grand Prix is held two weeks after his death and, fittingly, ends in a 1-2 finish for Ferrari.

1990s
COOLING
BRITANNIA

Despite kicking off in severe recession, the 90s are remembered as a period of relative optimism and prosperity. Around the globe there was a sense of growth and positive change. Communism collapsed in earnest, with infant democracies springing up in the former Soviet Union. George Bush Snr liberated Kuwait and left Saddam to his own devices for another decade. Not that he got up to much as it turns out.

This was the age when we went all technical, too, with the internet leaving the musty dungeons of IT nerds and growing deep roots in family homes around the world. The mobile phone followed a similar course, no longer the preserve of Brylcreemed yuppies, but instead a de-rigeur accessory for modern work and play.

Our cassettes had all morphed into CDs meanwhile, on which Grunge jostled for position with Girl Power. The Ladette had arrived, drinking more pints than the lads and knowing more of the words to *Don't Look Back in Anger*. New Labour checked in to Number 10 and we were, as a nation, immensely smug.

In hindsight, capitalism has ravaged Russia, the Middle East has become a polytunnel for terrorism, the internet is all porn and Facebook, the Ladettes have liver cirrhosis and we've stumbled blindly into the worst economic crisis in a century. But it wasn't all bad. We got the McLaren F1.

1990 **Vauxhall Lotus Carlton** ▶

For the uninitiated, there was little to distinguish the Lotus Carlton from the Vauxhall on which it was based. Underneath that still quite ordinary late-80s shell, however, lurked a formidable medley of GM performance parts, assembled and fine-tuned by Lotus to create the fastest saloon on early-90s Planet Earth.

Powered by a 377bhp, twin-turbo, 3.6-litre V6, the Lotus Carlton nudged 180mph and could hit 60mph in five seconds. The perfect getaway car, it was used regularly for just that purpose for many years to come.

1991 **Suzuki Cappuccino** ▶

Originally designed for Japan's 'Kei' class, with its focus on a compact footprint and low emissions, the Cappuccino was an unlikely gem from second-tier Japanese firm Suzuki. With its rear-wheel drive and excellent weight distribution, the tiny two-seater was surprisingly rapid for anyone willing to wring the life out of its fizzy 657cc engine. Cheap, quick and scary at the limit, this was midget muscle, so perfectly Japanese.

II February 1990

Although strictly an Oldsmobile man in his youth, Nelson Mandela switches allegiances as he is driven to freedom from Victor Verster prison in a Toyota Cressida.

1991 **Alpine A610** ▶

Although visually very similar to the Renault Alpine GTA, the A610 was a completely new car in every respect, with an enlarged and turbocharged engine now standard.

Tasked with significantly improving on its five-year-old forebear's rather middling fortunes, it was badged as an Alpine to increase the sporting appeal. Championed by an enthusiastic international press, uptake was still sluggish and after less than four years the last car to wear an Alpine badge ceased production.

1991 **LCC Rocket** ▶

Although the demand for weird and pricey track-day tools has exploded in the last few years, back in 1991 the Light Car Company's Rocket was a real curio. Drawn up by the legendary F1 designer Gordon Murray, the Rocket was a road-legal single-seater with a Yamaha superbike engine mounted behind the driver and optional tandem passenger.

Beautifully made and weighing less than 400kg, the Rocket mated motorbike acceleration to race-car cornering, and charged you £50,000 for the privilege.

1991 **Westfield SEight** ▼

The Westfield was a shameless rip-off of Caterham's Seven and universally regarded as the poor relation. When the Midlands firm shoehorned a 3.9-litre Rover V8 under its flimsy fibreglass bonnet, however, they suddenly had everyone's attention.

The SEight is a crude and terrifying creature with impossibly fast in-gear acceleration and an exhaust note to wake the dead. But, born of the same cottage industry insanity that gave us the AC Cobra, this sort of thing needs saluting. Preferably from a distance.

1991 **Bugatti EB110** ▼

Championed for reviving the Bugatti brand, albeit only for a moment, the £180,000 EB110 was the mother and father of all supercars when it appeared in 1991. Thanks to a radical carbon-fibre tub as well as a Gandini-designed all-aluminium body, four-wheel drive and a 550bhp, quad-turbo, 3.5-litre V12, 60mph was over and done with in 3.4 seconds, the limiter only reached at a truly horrifying 212mph.

1992 **Ford Escort RS Cosworth** ▶

The Holy Grail for a generation of rally fans and feral youth with face fuzz, the Escort Cosworth was another homologation special that allowed Ford to enter the World Rally Championship.

An impressive tally of wins on the WRC only added to the Cossie's street cred. Covered in vents and spoilers, the RS bristled with purposeful menace, backed up by a fierce turn of speed from its turbocharged Cosworth engine and four-wheel drive.

1992 **Porsche 928 GTS** ▶

The last of a long and illustrious line, the 928 GTS was the ultimate evocation of Porsche's luxury V8 GT. Originally conceived as a replacement for the 911, the front-engine 928 was a fully-loaded and immensely competent sporting grand tourer that was more comfortable, more refined and easier to drive than its twitchy stablemate.

The 1992 GTS took a 15-year-old design and threw everything Porsche had at it. Engine capacity was enlarged to 5.4-litres, with 350bhp at the rear wheels. Brakes were enlarged and the bodywork modified for improved aerodynamics. Despite a hefty kerbweight, the finely balanced GTS was a genuine performance tool with a five-second 0–60mph time and a top speed in excess of 170mph.

◀ 1992 **Renault Twingo**

One of the feistiest cars of the 90s was also one of the cheapest. The original Renault Twingo, with its 1.2-litre four-pot generating a mere 55bhp, was a firm favourite on the holiday hire market in western Europe, regularly seen taking winding coastal passes on the door handles, usually four up and always overdue a service by several thousand miles.

The Twingo was also a superbly packaged little city car, but the 'don't be gentle, it's rental' aphorism has given it far greater automotive significance.

1992 **BMW 850 CSi** ▶

Essentially the 'M' version of BMW's highly technical fat-cat express, the 850 CSi was the proper sporting option that devoted (and extremely wealthy) Beamer customers had been hankering after. Stiffer, lower, with a faster rack and wider stance, the CSi was only offered with a manual gearbox, mated to a mighty 375bhp, 5.6-litre V12. This was the sort of high-speed luxury transport normally reserved for the owners of private jets. Wring it out across a favourite B-road before crossing a continent on cruise control...

1992 **Jaguar XJR-15** ▶

A road-going development of Tom Walkinshaw's Le Mans-winning Silk Cut XJR-9, the 15 was a highly exclusive, massively expensive and little-known, mid-engined V12 supercar that was as close to driving a GT racer on the public road as you could get. Good for near enough 200mph and costing around half a million quid, this was seriously high-end stuff and only 50 were ever made.

What makes the XJR-15 even more significant, however, is the white elephant lurking in the wings in the shape of Jaguar's official, higher volume XJ220. Why would anyone want the XJ's V6 when they could have the championship-winning V12?

1992 **Subaru Impreza** ▶

A major milestone in modern rallying, the Impreza breathed new life into a workaday Japanese brand and made gods of various drivers on the WRC. In road trim it was available in a truly bewildering array of highly tuned and limited variants, but the original WRX STi, with its turbocharged, 247bhp, 2.0-litre boxer engine and permanent four-wheel drive was everything Subaru needed to do. Bomb-proof, indecently rapid and comparatively affordable, the STi defined performance motoring for the working man for well over a decade.

1992 **Porsche 964 RS** ▼

The late-80s 964 replaced the ageing 911 but was never as widely praised as the models that came before or indeed after, with one glorious exception. The 964 RS was an ultra-light, track-oriented version that harked back to the original 2.7 Carrera. With thinner glass, aluminium panels, new aero kit, no soundproofing, no stereo, no electric toys and no rear seats, this was a committed, competition-ready car that could be ordered in either touring trim or full-race spec with rear roll cage and stripped-out interior.

With its increased power, closer gear ratios and much stiffer suspension, the 964 RS was bit of a challenge to drive and an even bigger one to live with. Which didn't put anyone off for a second.

1992 **Ferrari 456 GT** ▶

Designed by Pininfarina at a time when Ferraris were all fairly outlandish, the 456 GT was a remarkably subtle and stylish statement of the marque's future intent. A generously proportioned 2+2 grand tourer, the 456 could whisk a family of four to nearly 190mph in cosseting, hand-stitched comfort. Although designed as a luxury touring car with all the space and refinements that Maranello's mid-engine offerings could not provide, the front-mounted, 5.5-litre V12 was good for 435bhp, putting the 456 second only to the F40 in terms of outright power.

This was to be the start of a genuinely practical and elegant line of ultra-modern GTs that has kept Ferrari's classier, more exclusive end up in the modern era of high-production volume and branded baseball caps.

1992 **Jaguar XJ220** ▼

The XJ220 was the stuff of dreams for the 90s schoolboy, with its sensual, futuristic outline promising unprecedented and ungodly levels of performance. More of a nightmare for both Jaguar and the hundreds of prospective punters who put down huge deposits, the XJ220 was originally conceived and marketed as an all-singing, four-wheel drive V12 with scissor doors and a top speed of 220mph, but due to financial constraints ended up with a turbo-charged V6, rear-wheel drive, normal doors and a top speed that should have seen it called the XJ213-ish. It was also vastly more expensive than provisionally estimated, causing a number of imminent owners to start legal proceedings against Jaguar.

They needn't have worried, however. The XJ220 was better off with its smaller, lighter and, as it turned out, more powerful engine, handled more sweetly with rear-wheel drive and was still the fastest production car on sale for several years.

1992 **Mitsubishi Lancer Evo 1 GSR** ▼

Originally only intended for its domestic market, the Lancer Evo 1 GSR quietly snuck over to the UK as a grey import and kicked off a 20-year national obsession with turning unbelievably boring, three-box saloons into rally-bred, four-door supercars. Created specifically to get Mitsubishi into the Group A rally series, the road-going derivatives were flimsy, rust-prone and a bit of a liability at their slightly unpredictable limits of adhesion. Imperfect when new and a far cry from the polished and highly technical Porsche-baiters of today, there is nevertheless something very special indeed about the rarer, rougher and marginally more subtle original that started it all.

19 March 1992

The Queen Mother purchases the last in a long line of Daimler limos from Jaguar, having been in love with the DS420 since 1970.

1992 McLaren F1

By the early 90s, the sharp end of the supercar market was awash with highly technical 200mph two-seaters. Gordon Murray, the moustachioed genius behind Brabham and McLaren's Formula 1 success, felt compelled to put an end to this automotive arms race by creating a car of such unimaginable speed and precision that everyone would simply have to throw in the towel. His vision was for a purely road-going, mid-engined sportscar, with bespoke V12 and carbon fibre monocoque, exactingly built in every possible respect to ensure day-to-day usability alongside utterly unprecedented levels of speed and handling. Easy.

In partnership with McLaren boss Ron Dennis, Murray set about it, and the upshot of this money-no-object enterprise was the F1, a car whose reputation both on road and racetrack remains completely unrivalled.

BMW was approached to supply the grunt, with its M-division's engine expert Paul Rosche presiding over the design and build of the 6.1-litre, V12 engine, housed amidships beneath a gold-foil heat shield to protect the carbon-fibre body. Power was rated at an astonishing 627bhp in road-going trim, which, against a kerbweight of just 1140kg, made the F1 faster than anything else that had gone before. Hitting 60mph in a whisker over three seconds and with a top speed of 240mph, 20 years on this remains the fastest normally aspirated car ever made.

Unsurprisingly, the F1, replete with McLaren Formula 1 technology and a unique central driving position, was quickly taken racing and utterly demolished the opposition at Le Mans in its debut year. With rule changes eventually rendering the F1 illegal in topflight competition, most of the GTR racers were simply converted back to road use, so rare and highly prized was the street-legal F1.

Today, with the limits of what is possible in engineering terms greatly increased, the McLaren F1 is still regarded by many designers and engineers as the performance benchmark. Gordon Murray achieved exactly what he set out to do: this really is the ultimate road car, past, present and future.

1993 De Tomaso Guara ▼

One of the least high-profile supercars of recent times, the De Tomaso Guara was built at the rate of about five a year for a decade. Sold as a coupé, convertible spider and totally al fresco barchetta, this was Alejandro De Tomaso's swansong, with production ceasing shortly after his death in 2003.

A guara is, apparently, a wild South American wolf, and De Tomaso's final offering, originally equipped with BMW's 304bhp, 4.0-litre V8 and bodied in lightweight Kevlar and fibreglass, lived up to the name with infamous high-speed handling habits.

1993 Lister Storm ▶

Its skills honed tweaking the Jaguar XJS in the 80s, Surrey-based tuner Lister began designing its own car to take on the mighty endurance-racing factory teams, built around a truly gigantic 7.0-litre V12 derived from Jaguar's Le Mans winning XJR.

Sadly, the chequered flag repeatedly eluded the unreliable Listers and its homologated street-legal version, a seriously intimidating melee of angles and bulges, was far too expensive considering its lack of provenance. A mere four road cars were ever built.

1993 **Porsche 968 Clubsport** ▾

Although a significant evolution of the ageing 944, the 968 continued the basic theme of a more affordable Porsche with favourable front-engined handling characteristics. Capitalising on this balance and predictability most effectively was the Clubsport, an ultra-light version of the standard 968 with a stripped-out interior and uprated suspension. It was much cheaper than the standard model and soon fêted as one of the purest driver's cars on sale. Its reputation is undiminished even today, making this Stuttgart's most desirable front-engined offering.

◀ 1993 **Toyota Supra**

The Mark IV Supra arrived in the UK in 1993, providing supercar levels of performance for a typically knockdown Toyota price. A far more sculptural affair than the previous angular incarnations, the new Supra was attractive in a muscular sort of way, a facet bolstered by the availability of a 320bhp, twin-turbo V6 that was capable of sub-five second 0–60mph times and a top speed of over 170mph.

The Supra was phased out after a decade but another 10 years on a replacement of sorts has finally made an appearance in the guise of the far less powerful GT86.

1993 **Wiesmann Roadster** ▶

Despite a very recent resurgence in the media, Weismann has been building its small and oddly-styled German roadster since 1993. Using BMW powertrains beneath fibreglass bodies, performance is predictably staggering, with incredible in-gear grunt now available through Beemer's super-slick SMG semi-auto gearbox.

Sadly both roadster and elegant coupé command six-figure sums nowadays, making the Weismann a hard sell against more familiar supercar fair.

1993 **TVR Griffith 500** ▶

Although most owners tend to remember the modern TVR through the mental equivalent of gritted teeth, the Griffith was and remains to this day an unusual highpoint. It was an instant classic in its beautiful simplicity of design and in any spec offered stomach-churning levels of performance.

The 500 was the one to have, however, with its 340bhp, 5.0-litre V8 able to take the fibre-glass roadster to 100mph in just over 10 seconds. Utterly unpredictable, in terms both of handling and on which days of the week it would start, the Griffith is still one of Blackpool's finest and an appreciating investment today.

1994 **Audi S8** ▶

There's something quite odd about the idea of a high-performance limousine. After all, if you're in the back seat reading spreadsheets and making important conference calls, chances are you could do without massive lateral G-forces and a ride quality that's shaking out your fillings. Nevertheless, the S8 was a triumph of extravagant, pointless performance, with every conceivable luxury whipped along by a 335bhp, 4.2-litre V8 and Quattro four-wheel drive. Super-stiff suspension has always made a bit of a mockery of the S8's executive status, but if you have a private plane to catch there are few more certain methods of making it.

17 June 1994

A white Ford Bronco becomes an international TV star when two dozen Los Angeles police cars and 20 news helicopters pursue former American Football star, actor and murder suspect O J Simpson along Interstate 405 in a bizarre slow-speed chase at just 35 mph.

1994 **Ferrari 355** ▶

Still considered one of Ferrari's most beautiful outlines in the modern era, the 355 is credited with ushering out Maranello's fashion for low-volume, high-anxiety supercars and replacing it with the sort of reliability and ease of use that customers were coming to expect.

You still had to pay Ferrari a fortune to completely remove the engine every time the cambelt needed changing – which is a lot in a high-performance Italian V8 – but at least, properly looked after, the F355 was near-as-dammit a daily driver.

1994 **Audi RS2** ▼

Turning its warp-speed, all-wheel drive expertise to more ordinary walks of motoring life, in the same year that Audi unveiled its executive S8 super saloon it also introduced the world's fastest family wagon. The RS2 was only ever sold as a five-door estate but, designed and built in conjunction with Porsche, it outperformed most sportscars on sale at the time.

Bigger turbo, bigger brakes and Porsche-tuned suspension made the RS2 a devastatingly effective cross-country tool.

With a 0–60mph time of 4.8 seconds and a top speed of over 160mph, this was hairy-toothed insanity dressed up as your cardigan-wearing neighbour from up the road.

1994 Marcos LM 500 ▶

Aiming to recapture some of its bygone sporting glory, Marcos reinvented itself in the mid-90s as a bona fide production line selling the fully built Mantara. To give it some much needed kudos, Marcos then homologated a series of Le Mans racing versions, calling them LMs and selling them in limited numbers to the public. Weighing next to nothing and powered by a 320bhp, 5.0-litre V8, the bulbous and be-winged road-going LM500 was as brutal to drive as it was to behold.

1995 Ferrari F50 ▼

Where the 288 GTO from the 80s had brought the potential of Group B racing to the road, the mid-nineties F50 attempted to do much the same with Formula 1.

This, on paper, sounds like a dangerous idea, all the more so when you learn that an enlarged version of the V12 from Ferrari's contemporary F1 car was mounted behind the driver in a car weighing just 1350kg. Using F1-derived suspension, with its total disregard for comfort, beneath a cramped and noisy cabin within a rigid, carbon-fibre tub, there was little to allay the fears of the presumably anxious (and now penniless) new owner.

Moreover, most of the F50's 520bhp really had to be wrung out from the high-revving V12, demanding real commitment and no shortage of bravery from driver and passenger alike.

This absolute lack of compromise is exactly what made the F40 great and, while not quite so highly regarded today, the F50 exists as an intriguing cautionary tale for F1 enthusiasts. Be careful what you wish for.

1995 **Renault Sport Spider** ▼

Having lost much of its sporting provenance in the late 80s and early 90s, the Sport Spider was designed as a halo car for Renault to inject a bit of vim into the rest of the range.

A very basic, stripped-out, mid-engined two-seater with no roof, nor even the pretence of one should it suddenly start bucketing, the Spider was an oddly impractical idea that only got away with it through tremendous handling characteristics. An aluminium chassis and composite bodywork ensured the Spider was very light, but the 148bhp engine never gave it quite the level of poke its focus, engineering and snappy styling deserved. Its fortunes received an almighty kick in the pants inside of a year anyway, when Lotus unveiled the vastly cheaper, faster and more practical Elise.

1995 **Venturi 400 GT** ▶

Based on the highly regarded but frustratingly unsuccessful Atlantique, the 400 GT was a road/race special that was sold in limited numbers by the French supercar firm Venturi. With its twin-turbocharged, 3.0-litre V6 generating 400bhp in road-going trim, the 180mph GT had all the performance to match its ground-hugging, race-bred styling.

Equipped with carbon ceramic brakes and the curious combination of a rollcage and full-leather interior, the 400GT blurred the boundaries between high street and pit lane like nothing France had seen before.

1995 **Volvo 850 T-5 R** ▶

Usually sporting a safe and sensible pair of brogues, on the odd occasion Volvo puts on its dancing shoes the results are astonishing. The 850 T-5 R was developed in conjunction with Porsche, using the already rapid, turbocharged T-5 as its starting point.

Sold in either black or a banana yellow – a colour developed for improved visibility – the T5-R dealt deftly with the paradox of high performance cosying up with world-beating levels of safety. Here was car that could hit 60mph in under six seconds, electronically limited to 155mph, that was also the first to provide an integrated child booster seat.

1995 **Porsche 993** ▼

Considered by the purists to be the last 'real' 911, the 993 was Porsche's final air-cooled flat-six, with its characteristic 'sit up and beg' driving position and typically Teutonic build quality. When the 993 bowed out after less than five years, the last real link with Stuttgart's original concept seemed to go with it. Nowadays a well-sorted 993 is worth far more than the 996 that replaced it, and high-performance variants like the Turbo and lightweight RS have become some of the most collectible Porsches in the world.

1995 **Renault Espace F1** ▼

The Renault Espace was Europe's first MPV, a slab-sided bus with all the sex-appeal of a dirty weekend in Woking. In 1995, to celebrate 10 years of building this functional, joyless shrine to family life and perhaps to gloss over the fact that Fred West and Harold Shipman had owned them, Renault decided to bolt an 800bhp V10 Formula 1 engine behind the driver's seat and rebody the entire thing in carbon fibre. The results were impressive. By supercar standards. The Espace F1 could very nearly reach 200mph and did the dash to 60mph in a backbreaking 2.8 seconds.

13 November 1995

An Aston Martin DB5 has an improbable tussle with a Ferrari F355 in the latest James Bond movie, Goldeneye. Without 007 behind the wheel, the Aston could never keep up...

1996 **Porsche 911 GT1** ▲

Hell-bent on another Le Mans victory, Porsche threw everything it had at an all-new 911-based sports prototype, the GT1. To meet with homologation rules for the FIA GT Championship, 25 road-going versions would be required. They cost half a million quid each and, despite a 544bhp twin-turbo, were only geared for 190mph and 0–60mph in four seconds. But this was a racing thoroughbred and, after 1998, a one-two Le Mans winner, that you could use to pop to the shops if you could find anywhere to keep your wallet.

◀ 1996 **TVR Cerbera**

At one point the fastest production car in the world, the gigantic, phallic, Cerbera was the white-knuckled apotheosis of TVR in the mid-90s. The first car to use TVR's in-house V8, it was furiously quick in any gear, an absolute nightmare to keep in a straight line and dogged by catastrophic unreliability. Nevertheless, this was the hairy-chested stuff that TVR was built on, with meaty, unassisted controls and a formidable reputation for punishing the inexpert. The Cerbera was as frightening to drive as it was to look at.

1996 **Lotus Elise** ▶

At the other end of the sports car spectrum from racecars costing a half-million quid was a far more significant game changer. The Lotus Elise first appeared in 1996, a raw but perfectly focussed, mid-engined, two-seater roadster. The Elise was cheap by sports car standards – and it needed to be considering how little it offered by way of creature comforts – but it was a true driver's car with superb balance, predictable handling and just enough poke to keep you coming back for more.

Using an aluminium tub, simple fibreglass body and out-sourced engine, the Elise would set a new template for Lotus and revive the firm's fortunes. This was just how Colin Chapman would have done it.

◀ 1996 **Porsche Boxster**

Derided by die-hard 911 aficionados, Porsche's soft-top Boxster was, in truth, fantastic, and in ways its bigger, rear-engined sibling could never be. The mid-engined configuration made it beautifully balanced, while its price point also made it far more affordable.

This was to be the start of a new and highly profitable era for Porsche, with water-cooled engines and extensive component sharing. The Boxster turned the low-volume Stuttgart specialist into a global phenomenon, proving the business model for the Cayenne SUV and ultimately evolving into the 911-bashing Cayman coupé.

◀ 1996 **Peugeot 406 Coupé**

Despite a pretty bad patch in the 90s, Peugeot did produce one of the finest affordable coupés in modern memory. The 406 was a sound but ordinary saloon, from which Italian design gurus Pininfarina designed, and in part assembled, the head-turning, two-door, four-seat coupé. Positive steering, predictable handling and a cracking choice of engines, including a sensible but gutsy diesel, offered the Average Joe an unprecedented slice of cut-price Italian exotica.

1997 **Subaru Impreza WRC** ▼

Subaru, already a dominant force on the international rally circuit, won the constructor's championship for the third year running with its 1997 Impreza WRC. This was the start of a new era of largely unrestricted prototypes that bore little relation to their road-going base models and did not require conventional homologation. The changes led to increasingly rapid cars demanding complicated and expensive development, and also bore witness to some of the truly great battles in World Rally history, with legends like Colin McRae and Richard Burns fighting Subaru's corner against the might of Ford and Citroën.

The Impreza won its debut at Monte Carlo and took a further seven victories in the inaugural season of the new WRC series, cementing Subaru's status as rallying royalty.

1997 **Peugeot 106 Rallye** ▶

The second generation 106 Rallye is arguably Peugeot's last great hot-hatch. A stripped-out, stiffened-up version of the Phase II hypermarche hero, the Rallye used the latter car's 1.6-litre engine with 103bhp tweaked out at a peak of 6,200rpm. Various timely improvements like power steering and an airbag helped make the Series 2 Rallye an easier car to live with, but this was always about rough-and-ready back-road blasts where its low weight, exceptional chassis and eager little engine made it a match for cars costing five times as much.

1997 **Nissan R390** ▼

Asked to name a high-performance Nissan, almost everyone able to give any sort of answer is going to say 'Skyline'. But in 1997 the Japanese firm took a proper punt at winning Le Mans by building a ground-up GT racer to compete in the top flight against Porsche and Mercedes-Benz. The R390 was developed in conjunction with Tom Walkinshaw, who had already cleaned up at Le Mans with the XJR-9 Jaguar. Its 3.5-litre V8 screamed out a massive 640bhp, enough to see it qualify ahead of all but the lead GT1 Porsche. Unfortunately, a dodgy gearbox denied Nissan any notable success on the track and only two road-going versions were ever built, ensuring the R390's near-total obscurity today.

1997 **Honda Integra Type R** ▼

A real rarity in the UK, but one that has a deeply loyal following, the 15-year-old Integra Type R still lays claim to being the greatest front-wheel drive performance car of all time.

Offering a raw and focussed driving experience only really akin to its contemporary Lotus Elise, the Type R was a paired-back version of Honda's uneventful three-door coupé, fitted with super-stiff sports suspension and a 187bhp, 4-cylinder, 1.8-litre engine that would rev to an ear-popping 8400rpm. Inside, Recaro bucket seats and slim aluminium gearknob were the only obvious reminders of what the Integra Type R was all about. And although good for 145mph and a 0–60 sprint of 4.5 seconds, it was the grip and handling that was untouchable then and remains the front-wheel drive benchmark to this day.

1998 **TVR Speed 12** ▶

The Speed 12 was a vast and truly terrifying melee of wings and spoilers. A one-off, road-legal racer, TVR had originally intended to enter it in the resurgent GT1 class at Le Mans, which meant building and selling a number of homologated versions for the DVLA to sweat about.

Based on the already staggeringly quick Cerbera, the Speed 12 was reputed to make around 900bhp from its 7.7-litre V12, in a car that tipped the scales at just over 1,000kg. Performance was never officially proven, but 60mph was expected to come up in under three seconds with a top speed in excess of 240mph.

Sadly, rule changes for Le Mans and 'development problems' saw the project stall despite the order book being full. But perhaps it's for the best that this £190,000 Le Mans-ready hyper-car never made it into Britain's showrooms. TVR's boss Peter Wheeler is reported to have driven a prototype home one night before declaring his own flagship model utterly unusable on the public road.

1998 **Nissan Skyline 400R** ▼

The fourth-generation R33 is the car that most people see in their mind's eye when they hear the word 'Skyline'. The 400R, however, is a rare beast indeed, built in strictly limited numbers and aggressively re-engineered by NISMO (Nissan Motorsport) to produce 400bhp in standard trim. A total engine overhaul, backed up by better cooling, brakes and vastly improved carbon-fibre aerodynamic aids, made the 400R a formidable adversary to the European supercar mainstays and a madcap tuner's paradise. Skylines can be, and with alarming regularity are, boosted to 1000bhp, making them as powerful as anything that has ever taken to the road.

4 July 1997

Who would want a remote-control car that did just one centimetre per second and cost $25 million? Answer – NASA, of course. The six-wheeled Sojourner is conducting experiments on the surface of Mars.

1998 Mercedes-Benz CLK GTR ▼

Not be outdone by the likes of McLaren and Porsche, Mercedes-Benz entered its CLK coupé into the 1997 FIA GT Championship, although this was not, strictly speaking, the CLK with which a late-90s punter would have been familiar. Built around a carbon-fibre and aluminium honeycomb monocoque with carbon-fibre panels, the CLK GTR was a five-metre long, two-metre wide, be-winged leviathan with a 612bhp, 7.0-litre V12 situated behind the tiny, up-front cockpit. In truth, the only thing it actually shared with the boggo CLK was the headlights.

Mercedes-Benz absolutely dominated the GT series, winning so easily in 1997 and 1998 that the competition all but dried up. Unsurprisingly, the 25 GTR road cars it had to build and sell for homologation quickly found owners, and that despite a price tag of £1 million.

1 January 1999

The Euro is launched onto the world's financial markets, meaning that a CLK GTR would set our mainland cousins back a hefty €1,420,000.

1999 **BMW Z3 M Coupé** ▼

The pretty and effeminate Z3 was soon found wanting by hardened BMW loyalists, criticised both for its lack of power and rigidity – a shortcoming frequent in roadsters. But a solution lay under wraps in BMW's design studio, one that would turn the soft and gentle ragtop into a fierce and focussed Munich masterpiece. The M Coupé used controversial bread-van styling to create a fixed-head Z3, and then threw in 320bhp from the standard, heavier M3. The result was a rigid and agile two-seater with a yammering straight-six and a tendency towards sudden and significant oversteer. From pretty and effeminate to ugly and manly, the M3 Coupé was a car that demanded your full attention from inside or kerbside, neither position proving terribly relaxing.

1999 **TVR Tuscan** ▶

Looking like something that had dropped off the undercarriage of a passing UFO, the TVR Tuscan appeared to a bewildered, but largely approving, public in 1999. It ushered in a new era of commendably daring and different design at the Blackpool factory, which concentrated as much on bonkers interiors as it did on otherworldly bodywork.

The Tuscan came with a characterful straight-six in various states of tune, any of which made it indecently fast – far quicker in any gear than ever seemed entirely safe. Utterly devoid of electronic driver aids and with not so much as an airbag to put in the way of the consequences, the Tuscan had a way about itself in the middle of a wet, high-speed corner that made men of boys and/or widows of their wives.

2000s
TERROR VS TOP GEAR TELLY

Riding a wave of socio-economic smugness, the West surfed into the noughties and promptly wiped out when the idol of its monetary magnificence, the World Trade Centre, went up in smoke. This was to be the decade characterised by THE WAR ON TERROR, a 21st-century crusade, the principal motivation for which was, allegedly, keeping petrol prices at an acceptable level for a society hooked on internal combustion.

On the flipside, sales of vegan sandals were going through the roof and the Toyota Prius became the flagship for hand-wringing environmentalists keen to make a slow-speed statement about the decade's other obsession: Climate Change.

Or should that be Reality TV? For a while we were meant to be panicking about Sarin nerve gas attacks or rising sea levels, instead whole countries began taking sabbaticals from actual reality to slump down in front of plasma-screen tellys bought on the never-never to watch 'ordinary' people making tits of themselves in the name of flash-in-the-pan celebrity.

And while we were all glued to a spittle-flecked, orange-skinned underclass clawing itself out of obscurity, China popped up as the next superpower, buying oil from pariah states and doing to the climate in a week what it took the UK a century to achieve.

Of far greater global significance, of course, was the reappearance of *Top Gear* in 2002. Changing the course of world history, or at least Sunday nights, three middle-aged men with dangerously poor dress sense and a flimsy grasp of the mechanical basics united families from pole to pole, dissolving the barriers of gender and class and curing the common cold. (Citation needed.)

They had a lot to go on, though. The 2000s was a veritable treasure trove of motoring booty, with the mighty marques of Porsche, Lamborghini, Aston Martin and Ferrari denying our inexorable progress towards a zero-emissions future with a cavalcade of V8 and V12s. This really was the end of an era, celebrated in aptly indulgent and ridiculous style.

2000 **Noble M12** ▶

A fitting way to start the decade, the Noble M12 GTO appeared to reassure the motoring public that the quintessentially British art of building, quite badly, very fetching and very fast plastic sports cars in remote rural sheds was still in rude health.

The M12 looked like a boil-washed Le Mans racer with its fibreglass clam shells and massive rear wing, and inside, where everything down to the standard rollcage was trimmed in Alcantara, you could hear the constant rasp and whine of twin turbochargers mated to a Ford-sourced, 3.0-litre V6. It was expensive, almost never started and made you look like a bit of prat on the rare occasions that it did, but this was and still is exactly what plucky British engineering is all about.

2000 **Lotus 340R** ▼

Originally intended solely as an attention-grabbing show car, the 340R was a no-holds-barred take on the already unforgiving and far from luxurious Lotus Elise. With no roof, windscreen, windows or doors, the 340R pared back everything that even the most masochistic performance purist would deem necessary and eventually sold it to a salivating public for an awful lot more than its regular counterpart.

Hot, wet, noisy and £35,000, the 340R was a lunatic indulgence that made up for its absurdity with impeccable balance and magnetic levels of mid-corner grip.

2000 BMW Z8 ▲

In homage to the glorious mid-50s 507, BMW greeted the new millennium with a highly limited two-seat roadster, bodied in hand-made aluminium and powered by the 400bhp, 5.0-litre V8 from its M5 saloon.

Full of convincing echoes of its former glories, including a fabulously retro interior, the Z8 was truly beautiful to behold and thanks to low weight and masses of grip, devastatingly quick in a straight line. With a traditional front-engined, rear-drive layout and meaty manual gearbox, it wasn't quite a handling match for its more technical Italian mid-engined rivals, but its old-school styling and modern muscle have made it an absolute classic.

2000 Saleen S7 ▶

Although Americans are widely, and quite rightly, ridiculed for most of the detritus they manufacture in the name of motoring, there are some monumental exceptions. The Saleen S7 is a serious knee-trembler of a thing, all fins and slats and scissor doors, with a massive, 7.0-litre V8 mid-mounted and putting out 550bhp.

Perhaps unsurprisingly, the 200mph top speed didn't cut it for long, and five years later a 750bhp twin-turbo version appeared with a claimed top speed of 248mph. And few volunteers to prove it.

2000 **Lotus Exige** ▼

The next in a long line of performance leg-ups for the Elise, the brutal, track-bred Exige took the already uncompromising roadster and turned it into a pocket GT racer.

Dramatic but deliberate aerodynamic improvements, including a fastback rear panel, ground-hugging chin-spoiler, rear wing and air scoop on the newly fixed roof, gave the Exige a real sense of purpose. And this was matched by a significant performance hike from the standard 1.8-litre Rover K-Series engine, now tuned to within in an inch of its wheezy little life at up to 192bhp.

Although never about outright speed, to this day there is almost nothing on earth that can hang onto the Exige's coattails through a series of fast, tight corners. As road-legal racers go, there was none cheaper, better looking nor more capable of turning your hour-long commute into a little slice of Le Mans.

2000 **Volkswagen Lupo GTI** ▶

With the demands both of safety and luxury expanding the size and weight of cars to a dynamically detrimental extent, Volkswagen's Golf GTI was a shadow of its lithe and agile former self by the year 2000.

Which is where the little Lupo came in. Wedging the 1.6-litre unit from the Polo under its tiny bonnet and tweaking it up to 125bhp, VW created an unlikely gem in the new GTI that was widely hailed as the spiritual successor to the original hot hatch. Ridiculous but glorious, Wolfsburg's bionic baby was indecently quick and looked the business.

2000 **Ford Racing Puma** ▶

Based on its bland but competent standard coupé, Ford developed another showcase for its performance know-how with the Racing Puma. This was a halo car, built in limited numbers and sold at a loss to pump a bit of performance kudos back into the whole brand.

Only 500 Racing Pumas were ever produced, reputedly because a high price knobbled demand. Which is a shame, because there was a bit of magic here. The track was widened, with flared arches made of lightweight aluminium. Stiffer springs improved road holding while bigger brakes increased stopping power for the uprated 153bhp engine. Although not particularly fast, the grippy and predictable Racing Puma was hugely involving. Finding a good one today is a challenge, though. Scarce in the first place, too many have been modified and driven into the ground.

2001 **Volkswagen Passat W8** ▶

The Passat W8 brought with it two world firsts. The engine was a pair of four-cylinder 'Vs' bolted together to make a small, compact 8-cylinder. And the W8 was that strangest of things, a really expensive Volkswagen. An unlikely rival for the established performance saloons from Mercedes-Benz and BMW, the £30,000 W8 put 275bhp to all four wheels, providing a 0–60mph time of 6.8 seconds and electronically limited top speed of 155mph.

A moment of inspired madness from the perennially sensible VW, the rare and innocuous W8 is one of the great 'Q' cars of all time.

2001 **Renaultsport Clio V6** ▶

The Renaultsport Clio V6 was the car every motoring writer wanted first dibs on when it appeared in 2001, and the one few dared go anywhere near after performing their first involuntary mid-corner pirouette. With a 3.0-litre V6 where the rear seats were meant to be, sending 230bhp to the rear in a car with a tiny wheelbase, the scope for launch-day carnage was almost limitless.

Just two years later Renault whisked up an extensively re-engineered replacement that successful dialled out the death-wish cornering and made more of the engine through tuning and gearing. It was still a tricky beast, mind you, but the bit was finally in its teeth.

2001 **Honda Civic Type R** ▼

The second generation Civic Type R did more to establish Honda's performance credentials in the UK than even the mid-engined NSX supercar. An instant classic thanks to an uncompromising ride, maniacally free-revving 2.0-litre engine and snappy gear change from a dash-mounted manual box, the Type R was a dangerously addictive alternative to the plobby and predictable Golf GTI.

2001 **Skoda Superb** ▶

Borrowing from its pre-war lineage, Skoda rather boldly dubbed its re-badged Passat the Superb. But it had a point. With an extended wheelbase providing limo-like levels of rear legroom and an inherited Germanic solidity that exploded all the Cold War myths about the Czech firm's quality control, the Superb was just that. And it was yours for half the money of the established executive big boys from Germany.

All the better for a revision in 2008, the Superb has made repeated mockery of the badge politics that pervades its market segment. Skoda is the anti-brand, the Superb its excellent, reluctant flagship.

2001 **Westfield XTR2** ▼

Straying from its sub-Caterham roots, Westfield unveiled the XTR2 in 2001, a road-legal track day tool that looked for all the world like a miniature prototype class Le Mans racer.

Powered by a Suzuki superbike engine that delivered its peak power at a screaming 9,800rpm through a six-speed sequential gearbox, the XTR2 was a demanding and technical bit of kit that required both delicacy of touch and balls of steel to really exploit.

At one point the fastest car round *Top Gear*'s track, knocking the Pagani Zonda off pole in the process, the XTR2 only cost £20,000 and you could build it in your shed.

6 July 2001

BMW unveil the new Mini, 42 years after its iconic older brother first rolled off the production line.

◄ 2001 **Aston Martin Vanquish**

The last of the old world Astons, the Vanquish was a glorious farewell to the marque's low-volume, hand-built production line at Newport Pagnell.

This was no dinosaur, however. Underneath that angular, muscular body was a highly advanced and complex bonded and extruded aluminium chassis. Bolted to this was a 460bhp, 6.0–litre V12 mated in-turn to a problematic six-speed paddle-shift gearbox.

In later 'S' form the Vanquish became a genuine 200mph supercar and one with significantly improved handling. Costing around £165,000 new, nowadays this milestone in British engineering can be picked up for the price of an Audi RS5, with all the niggles ironed out at someone else's expense.

2002 **Farboud GTS** ▶

The brainchild of a wealthy young playboy, the GTS was actually a far more serious contender than most in the shed-built supercar market. Glorious to look at and replete with the best-possible bespoke performance parts, Arash Farboud's mid-engined, twin-turbo 911-baiter really deserved the limited production run that ultimately eluded it.

Ten years later, however, justice was done. Sort of. The GTS has finally made the showrooms, revised and re-badged as the Ginetta G60.

2002 **Volkswagen 1-Litre** ▼

A glimpse into our motoring tomorrow, albeit already an astonishing 10 years old, the Volkswagen 1-Litre was conceived as a test bed for fuel efficiency, concentrating primarily on super-slippery aerodynamics. Bodied in carbon fibre over a magnesium-alloy chassis, the 1-Litre sat two in tandem and dispensed with external clutter like wing mirrors in favour of tiny rear-facing cameras. Powered by a modest, 299cc, single-cylinder diesel engine, VW's road-legal eco warrior managed to travel 100km on a single litre of fuel, the equivalent of 235mpg.

◀ 2002 **Daihatsu Copen**

A guilty pleasure for many a hairy-chested motoring hack, the Copen was a surprisingly involving and useable two-seat sports car that made an addictive virtue of its minute proportions and power train.

With its retro/futuristic styling and ingeniously compact folding tin-top, the Copen looked the part, and when its fizzy little engine was on song it had a remarkable turn of speed.

19 February 2002

Ford brings 90 years of car production in Britain to a close when the final Fiesta rolls off the Dagenham production line just one month after the company announced its new model Fiesta will be produced in Spain.

2002 **Volkswagen Phaeton** ▶

A lesson learned for the huge and self-confident German uber-brand: nobody wants an executive limousine with a Volkswagen badge on the bonnet. Which is daft, on reflection, because the Phaeton was a tour de force of luxury and innovation that made the established Mercedes-Benz S-Class look overpriced and under-equipped by comparison.

Available with an all-new W12 engine and a list as long as your arm of luxury on-board gizmos, the Phaeton nevertheless failed to make any sort of impression on the UK market. A ruinous investment new, these are now a seriously shrewd second-hand buy for the penny-pinching big cheese.

2002 **Suzuki Liana** ▶

The Liana went from zero to hero in 2002 after it became the first of *Top Gear*'s reasonably priced cars. Run ragged on a weekly basis by cussing, sweating celebrities, this cut-price Japanese saloon took more punishment than a blind boxer, covering an estimated 1,600 laps of the track before being retired in favour of the equally awful Chevrolet Lacetti.

2002 **Ferrari Enzo** ▼

As a fitting homage to the late, great main man, Ferrari set about making what was, for a fleeting moment, the ultimate supercar. With form following function and, in its own way, finding form again, the Enzo was a beautiful brute, with its wingless but highly aerodynamic bodywork, wide stance and close, protruding cockpit.

Behind the driver a brand-new, 650bhp V12 would rip the Enzo to 60mph in a fraction over three seconds and only run out of steam at 220mph. Using a variety of F1 technologies while exploiting additional advances like adaptive aerodynamics that were banned in the sport, the Enzo offered the best of both worlds. But only to 400 people, all of whom had to cough up £450,000.

2002 **Aston Martin DB7 Vantage Zagato** ▶

Forever praised for its elegant lines and, perhaps more importantly, for steadying Aston Martin's yo-yoing fortunes, the DB7 was, nevertheless a bit of a wet fish. Made of steel where Aston predominantly preferred lighter aluminium, and powered by a 3.0-litre straight-six when Aston was already pedalling a mighty V8 in the Virage, this was a modern, mass-production car that lacked the heritage and bespoke quality the firm's devotees had come to expect.

Redressing all this fell, as it often does, to Zagato. Using the far more convincing, 6.0-litre V12 from the Vantage and placing it on a shortened chassis, the Milanese coachworkers then carved out a sculptural aluminium body. Adding exclusivity to the mix, only 99 Vantage Zagatos were ever made, all of them snapped up for silly money in minutes.

2002 **Ford Focus RS** ▶

The original Focus was swamped with praise for its chassis and steering, making it the natural starting point for another low-volume, high-performance variant. The RS looked the part, beefed up with flared arches over a wider track and heavily ventilated front spoiler, while underneath a racing clutch and limited slip diff were drafted in to cope with a turbocharged 212bhp. Precise, predictable and ideally powered for a B-road hack, this remains one of the best front-wheel drive performance cars of all time.

2002 **Honda NSX Type R** ▶

While the slow-selling Honda NSX had attracted attention and praise for its polish and usability, it was now over a decade old. Determined to wring the last from its superb mid-engined design and tuneable, 3.2-litre V6, Honda released a highly limited Type R version that dispensed with almost every road-going luxury to create a far lighter, track-focussed variant. The result was a punishing semi-competition car that was a match for far newer and more powerful exotica, if you could put up with the noise and the teeth-loosening ride. The NSX bowed out in typically no-nonsense style.

2002 **Lamborghini Murcielago**

The Murcielago marked the moment when Lamborghini became a bona fide global force. It had been over a decade since the distinctly old-school Diablo appeared and in that time the firm had entered the gigantic family fold of the Volkswagen Audi Group. This meant enough funding, technological know-how and parts sharing to put Lamborghini at the forefront of the supercar space race.

The Murcielago was a truly gob-smacking piece of design. Hugely wide and improbably low, it seemed pinned to the ground by high-speed downforce, even standing still. Behind the driver, a 6.2-litre V12 bellowed its way to a peak power of 576bhp at 7500rpm while beneath him Audi's world-beating four-wheel drive system kept everything in a straight line – the most remarkable thing about this extraordinary 210mph supercar being just how tractable it was.

Safe, functional and, thanks to its German godparents, utterly reliable, it was still no treat to parallel park on a busy street but this was a Lambo you could really live with. The Murcielago proved that you could have the drama of supercar ownership without the attendant angst, shifting the goal posts for every future performance car.

2003 **Mazda RX-8** ▶

Every decade or so Mazda feels the urge for another Wankel. Perhaps its most convincing effort at a rotary engine to date, the RX-8 was a promising blend of free-revving performance, futuristic styling and a practical four-seat configuration.

Hampered by oil consumption second only to its thirst for fuel, the RX-8 was a little too expensive and tricky to run, but its ingenious suicide rear doors and proper second row of seats made this the go-to car for a family man with a need for speed.

2003 **Kamaz 49111** ▼

For years Russian truck-maker Kamaz has completely dominated the Dakar Rally, where biblically vast and fast four-wheel drive lorries are raced for two weeks solid through the extreme heat of desert dunes in Africa and South America.

The Kamaz 49111 was raced almost as it would have left the factory, but for a twin-turbocharged diesel V8 now developing over 800bhp. Modified only to keep up with the FIA's ever-changing regulations, the Kamaz has now won the Dakar an astonishing 10 times.

2003 **MG SV** ▾

MG's late-90s resurgence peaked here, with the SV. This would be the marque's first real punt at proper performance, an all-carbon-fibre bodied, front-mid-engined V8 supercar with 320bhp on tap and a top speed of 165mph. A low-volume loss leader, the SV was meant to be a sort of ultra-exclusive, bespoke product a bit like earlier Aston Martins. You pay up, then help with development. The list price was £75,000 though, an awful lot for an MG, especially one that was half-finished. Unsurprising then that the SV never made it. But what might have been?

◀ 2003 **Vauxhaull VX220 Turbo**

As a re-bodied Lotus Elise, the Vauxhall VX220 was a bit of a disappointment. Less kerb appeal, too much understeer and, worst of all, a Vauxhall badge. But the addition of a turbocharger to this lightweight, mid-engined roadster completely rewrote the rules. Now the VX220 could hit 60mph in under five seconds and pass 150mph, becoming an affordable little giant-killer over a familiar twisting back road.

2003 Mitsubishi Lancer Evo VIII FQ-400 ▼

Translating hard-won performance expertise from the world rally circuit to its cheap and cheerless four-door saloon, Mitsubishi continued to create some of the fastest road cars available at any price. The Evo VIII FQ-400 managed to squeeze over 400bhp from its 2.0-litre, four-cylinder engine, enabling it to hit 60mph in three seconds dead and only run out of steam at 175mph. This made it as fast in a straight line as many supercars costing two or three times the price, and on a challenging country road there was nothing that could touch it.

2003 Wiesmann GT MF4 ▶

Building on the modest, ultra-low volume success of its no-expense spared roadster, in 2003 Wiesmann unveiled a far better-looking fastback fixed-head GT. Powered by a 362bhp twin-turbo V8 sourced from BMW and paring back the pounds with a lightweight, Elise-style aluminium tub beneath composite bodywork, the GT was as fast and capable as it was exactingly built and finished. Expensive and seriously rare, these are high-end classics the minute they leave the factory.

2003 **Dodge Viper** ▼

Despite a decade of production Stateside, it wasn't until 2003 that the Viper, known as the SRT-10 in its third iteration, made it to the UK as an official import. Major design improvements over the shockingly agricultural original couldn't make up for the new Viper still only being available in left-hand drive, or for it being blessed with all the refinement (and the drivetrain) of an HGV. It remained, regardless, the last word in American muscle, with its 8.3-litre V10 putting out 500bhp and a devastating 525 lb ft of torque.

2003 **Ferrari 575 Maranello** ▶

The 575 was a stepping stone between the less than brilliant 550 Maranello on which it was based and the entirely brilliant 599 GTB with which it shared almost nothing.

This was a period of radical reinvention for Ferrari as it embraced the age of computer design with an enthusiastic Italian hug. So the 575 Maranello featured various significant advances like the first 'F1' paddle shift on a V12 and clever adaptive suspension. Its bodywork, meanwhile, was the beneficiary of subtle but significant improvements in aerodynamics over the 550, and a 'GTC' handling pack was now available that added ceramic brakes and stiffer, sportier suspension.

The 575 was a sizeable step forward then, with greatly improved agility and a potential top speed of 203mph. But in less than four years it would be obsolete, an also-ran of the analogue age.

Funded, badged and powered by Mercedes-Benz but built in Woking by McLaren, the SLR was a technological tour de force that borrowed extensively from Formula 1 to create the ultimate sporting grand tourer. Underneath that truly enormous bonnet lay a hand-built, AMG, 5.5-litre V8 making over 600bhp. With active aerodynamics on its all-carbon body, massive ceramic brakes and ingenious inventions like 'Sensotronic' brakes that calculate the optimum braking pressure for each wheel, no expense was spared in the development of the SLR. It was never quite the sum of its parts, however. There were more comfortable and vastly more affordable GTs out there, and infinitely better out-and-out sports car. But the SLR was a benchmark for the noughties, a fist thumping, 200mph statement of Merc's luxurious, high-tech, high-performance prowess.

30 July 2003

The familiar stutter of the air-cooled flat-four is heard for the last time at Volkswagen's Puebla plant in Mexico when Type 1 VW number 21,529,464 becomes the final Beetle to be built, ending a production run of 58 years. The last car is shipped off to the VW museum in Wolfsburg.

2004 **VW Race Touareg** ▼

Dominating the Dakar for exactly as long as the funding kept coming, the fast, frugal and immensely high-tech Race Touareg was Volkswagen's unique and eye-wateringly expensive way of enlightening the world as to the brilliance of its TDI diesel engines. Breathtakingly quick over any given terrain but, more importantly, easy on the fuel and utterly dependable, the carbon-fibre bodied, all-wheel drive Race Touaregs were driven to three back-to-back victories across the deserts and mountains of South America. Job done, point made, VW abandoned the Dakar and has since set its sights on the WRC.

2004 **Subaru Forester STi** ▶

For reasons best known to themselves, the bigwigs at Subaru decided not to export the Forester STi to the UK, despite the fact that a significant percentage of the British population were Impreza loyalists with burgeoning family commitments.

The Forester STi was a practical, sensible, small SUV with a 261bhp flat-four capable of hauling it to 60mph in under seven seconds. With a bomb-proof build and cavernous boot, it struck a sly balance between performance and functionality, offering a last ray of hope to the expectant father with his Scooby already in the small ads.

2004 **Morgan Roadster** ▼

We could've stuck the Morgan anywhere in this book and it would've been pretty much the same: steel chassis, hand-carved ash frame – surprisingly good in a crash apparently – old-school aluminium bodywork and a homegrown engine. What makes the flagship Roadster noteworthy is that this is the moment when Morgan gave up the long-running, Rover-powered Plus-8 in favour of a far more modern Ford V6. After over 30 years the new 3.0-litre Duratec made the Morgan more frugal and dependable without compromising on its flies-in-teeth performance. The tiny Malvern firm had entered the new millennium. In a manner of speaking.

16 November 2004
In an age when no self-respecting supercar would admit to a top speed of less than 200mph, NASA's unmanned Scramjet aircraft hits 7,000mph – almost ten times the speed of sound.

2004 **Cadillac CTS-V** ▶

Cadillac has never made much of an impression on the UK, perhaps because we didn't want overpriced, dynamically redundant saloons with slushy auto 'boxes and all the class of a pimp's thong.

The CTS-V attempted to speak our language, however. Here was a mid-sized saloon with track-tuned suspension, a six-speed manual gearbox and BMW M5-rivalling levels of power. That supercharged, 6.2-litre V8 made 550bhp, good for a claimed top speed of 191mph, and although well short of the precision of an M5 or E-Class AMG, it had enough character to tempt a few buyers from the anodyne European alternatives.

2004 **Bristol Fighter** ▶

In what may well have been Bristol's last-gasp attempt to stay relevant in an age it no longer understood, it released the Fighter in 2004 with characteristically little fanfare and absolutely no involvement from the awaiting media.

Shipped off discreetly to its secretive and very wealthy clientele, the Fighter broke with ancient Bristol tradition as a gull-winged, two-seat supercar. The massive Chrysler engine was still in situ however, this one the 8.3-litre V10 from the Dodge Viper, rebuilt to Bristol's exacting, aeronautical grade specifications.

The car cost £235,000 and claimed a top speed of 210mph, rising to 225mph in its later turbocharged form. Rarer than Jesus, no-one can get their hands on one to find out if it's true.

◀ 2004 **Chrysler ME Four-Twelve**

Chrysler in the 21st century has been responsible for some Class 1 turd – think ditchwater Sebring or retro-carbuncle PT Cruiser – but it revealed in 2004 a remarkable ability for polishing the aforementioned.

The ME Four-Twelve, short for Mid-Engine, Four-turbo, Twelve-cylinder, was a strikingly beautiful carbon fibre concept, devised in-house and then dangled before the world's media as production viable.

With 850bhp from its Mercedes-Benz-sourced, all-aluminium V12 AMG engine, the ME Four-Twelve was theoretically capable of hitting 60mph in under three seconds and reaching 248mph. Unsurprisingly, Chrysler's very own Veyron never quite made it into the brochure, but we all appreciated the fleeting fancy.

2004 **Aston Martin DB9** ▶

The DB9 marked the beginning of a new era for Aston Martin, one of high-tech factory lines, high-volume production and, God forbid, something like profitability. But, in many respects, this was familiar stuff. With a huge engine up front in a luxuriously appointed 2+2, the DB9 was traditional grand touring at its modern best.

Extremely expensive but neither as capable nor as quick as its rivals from Ferrari or Porsche, the new 470bhp V12 Aston, with its six-speed auto gearbox and indifference to headline performance figures, maintained a dignified distance from the nouveau riche exotica it was supposedly up against.

2004 **Volkswagen Golf GTI** ▼

Almost 30 years after the original GTI and some fairly awful evolutions inbetween, Volkswagen finally got round to building another Golf worthy of its own hallowed moniker.

The Mk V GTI was a truly astonishing car, with exceptional refinement, quality and practicality alongside perfectly judged retro/modern styling and peerless hot-hatch performance. This was a complete package in every sense. And never mind its niche dominance, in the right hands on a tricky road there was nothing this side of a Porsche 911 Turbo that could keep up with the GTI. Real brilliance comes along so rarely in a motoring lifetime and this was most definitely it.

2004 Invicta S1 ▼

Hand-built to exacting standards with a super-strong chassis and the world's first one-piece carbon-fibre body, the Invicta S1 should have been brilliant, and in many respects it was. Supple ride, agile handling, impressive interior luxury and a meaty, 320bhp V8 all added up to a compelling, if slightly weird-looking, package. But the grim reality of building supercars in sheds is that there are very few people who want to part with a six-figure sum for weird-looking packages, especially ones their Porsche-driving friends have never heard of.

2004 Maserati Gransport ▶

Spurred on perhaps by the imminent arrival of its shiny new MC12, Maserati set about sorting the near-miss 3200GT in 2004. Called the Gransport, this subtle but skilful development turned a twitchy GT into a more mature and convincing performance thoroughbred. Power was up, suspension sorted and the much-criticised semi-auto gearbox 35 per cent faster in the changes. A genuine 911 rival at last, and with bags more character.

2004 **Maserati MC12** ▼

With Maserati and Ferrari now jointly owned by Fiat, the opportunity to gift Maser with a flagship supercar borrowing the best bits from its one-time rival was too good to miss. The MC12 used the ingenuity and engine from the Ferrari Enzo and was sold in incredibly limited numbers to allow Maserati to take part in the FIA GT Championship. Which it won with ease, although the massive and claustrophobic road car was virtually undriveable.

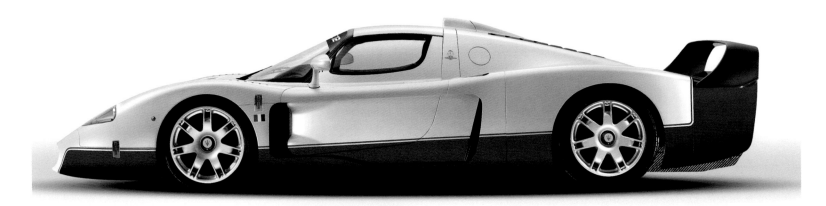

◄ 2004 **Mercedes-Benz CLS 320 CDI**

When Mercedes-Benz launched the CLS in 2004, it lit the touchpaper for design studios everywhere. Suddenly, a four-door saloon was a bit last season, a coupé trying too hard. The CLS was the first of an increasing range of elegantly styled yet just about still practical four-door coupés, the best of which was not the massively fast and expensive AMG version, but the humble, frugal and serene 320 CDI diesel. A joy to look at, a joy to drive, as a union of form and function this was getting on for perfection.

◄ 2004 **Jaguar XKR-R**

After eight years of production the original XK8, never a real performance car in the first place, was looking a little blunt of claw. Some concerted sharpening was undertaken however, by way of the XKR-R. A one-off build that showcased the performance potential Jaguar couldn't make a business case for, the 'R' was a ground-up rebuild with a massively stiffer chassis, limited slip diff, huge brakes, a manual gearbox and more aggressive and aerodynamic bodywork. Over 400bhp was squeezed out of the 4.0-litre V8, too, shoving it to 60mph in 4.6 seconds and all the way to 180mph. And they even threw in a place to keep your crash helmet.

◀ 2004 **Maserati Quattroporte**

Picking up a baton Maserati had first run with some 40 years before, the Quattroporte reappeared for the fourth time in 2004, this time as a beautiful but highly capable sporting saloon that struck a compelling balance between dignified executive transport and addictive, sonorous performance.

Using a 4.2-litre V8 in a front/mid-engine position, the Pininfarina-penned Quattoporte was a triumph, both dynamically and aesthetically, making the Mercedes-Benz S-Class and BMW 7-Series look impossibly boring by comparison.

2004 **BMW M3 CSL** ▼

Four years into production, BMW took one of the most affordable and tractable high-performance cars on sale and made it hugely expensive and almost undriveable. In doing so they created a modern classic. The CSL was a lightened, stiffened M3 with more power and the fastest semi-auto gearbox the world had seen. Screaming like a banshee and shaking out your molars, the Spartan, carbon-roofed CSL was a zero-compromise track tool with a tax disc. And it would set you back as much as a Porsche 911.

2004 **Porsche Carrera GT**

Having invested heavily in a stalled Le Mans racing project, Porsche found itself using one of the great performance engines of the modern era as a coffee table. By the time it was wiped down and mounted amidships in the carbon-fibre monocoque of the Carrera GT, this 5.7-litre V10 was howling out over 600bhp, all of it at the rear wheels via a six-speed manual gearbox and twin-plate ceramic clutch.

This was a fearsome thing then, full of unforgiving racing DNA, intended for the highest levels of motorsport and its attendant skill set. Where its principal rival, the Ferrari Enzo, offered a smorgasbord of on-board computer wizardry to flatter the driver, the Carrera GT extolled the virtues of less as more. This was all about exacting engineering, raw power and the sort of driver who knew how to handle it.

Sold into the feverish, unsuspecting grasp of Porsche Public, it's no surprise that several soon came a cropper in monumental fashion, but driven with the expertise it clearly demanded, the Carrera GT quickly established itself as one of the all-time greats. At the Nürburgring's infamous Nordschleife, a circuit so dangerous it was banned from top-flight motorsport back in the 70s, Porsche's new flagship held the road-legal lap record over the lethal 13 miles of twists and jumps for over three years.

Where even the most exotic of supercars come and go, history will remember the Carrera GT; for its purity of purpose, for its timeless beauty and for its admonishment of the over-eager amateur.

2005 Ferrari FXX ▼

For anyone unfulfilled by the exclusivity and performance of their Enzo, help, of a sort, was at hand. Twenty mega-wealthy owners were offered the 'opportunity' to buy an FXX, an Enzo-based hypercar that was neither road legal nor eligible for competition.

This was classic Ferrari, getting its punters to contribute towards its glorious future by allowing them to buy into its own research and development. They would become test drivers, or at least that's what Ferrari would tell them as they handed over their 1.5 million Euro cheques. The FXX was a bewildering vision of high-tech wings and spoilers, a ridiculous warp-speed test mule that offered its handful of owners a ruinous but remarkable privilege. Its Enzo-based engine was now running near 800bhp with a top speed of over 240mph. Ferrari said when and where the FXX would be driven – only at closed test tracks and circuits – and then sat back to watch the mayhem.

2005 BMW M6 ▶

The 6-Series has always been a bit of an oddball for BMW. Not great to look at, not as practical as the 5-Series and lacking the performance to lure people away from the default sporting GT, the Porsche 911.

A quick call to M Sport sorted most this out, however. Now the 6-Series had the monster V10 from the M5 as well as its Jekyll and Hyde 'Sport' button and lightning-quick SMG paddle-shift gearbox. With 501bhp available at an eye-watering 7750rpm, the M6 was supercar rapid, but still had the refined and tractable characteristics of a high-end GT.

The looks remained divisive, but from the driver's seat you didn't have time to care.

2005 **Ford GT** ▼

In a road-oriented sequel to the mighty Le Mans showdowns of the 60s, Ford decided to take Ferrari on at its own game in 2005. The GT was heavily influenced by the looks of the all-conquering GT40 endurance racer, but this wholly modern homage was every inch a match for the contemporary Ferrari 360 road car.

Using a mid-mounted, 550bhp, 5.4-litre V8 and aluminium body, the huge and beautiful GT was devastatingly quick in any gear, bursting with old-school Detroit character and good for 205mph. It had one major flaw, however, and that was a raging thirst. Owners were lucky to get to off their own front drives without having to find a petrol station on the way.

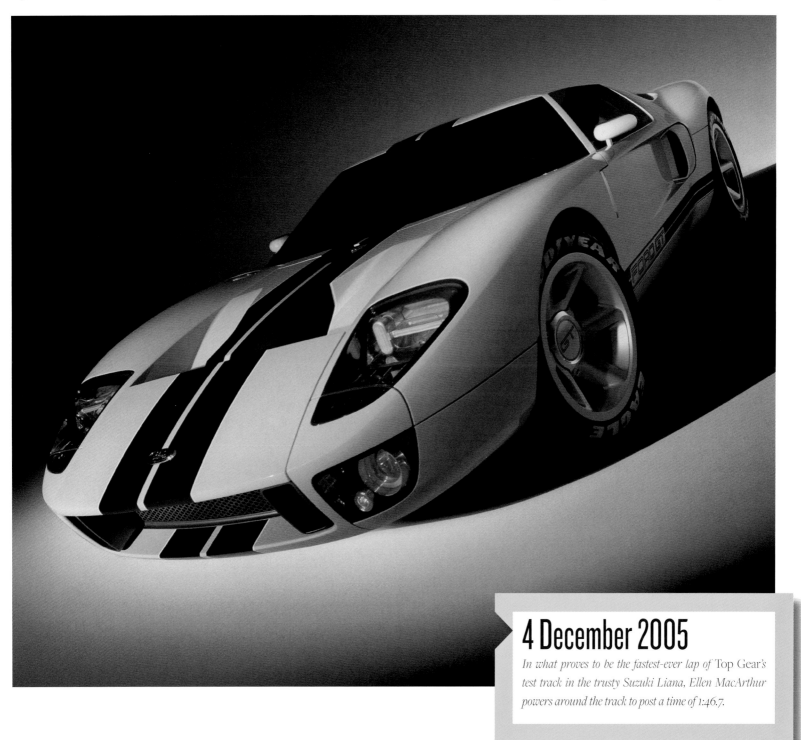

4 December 2005

In what proves to be the fastest-ever lap of Top Gear's test track in the trusty Suzuki Liana, Ellen MacArthur powers around the track to post a time of 1:46.7.

2005 **Gumpert Apollo** ▼

In that exotic niche where cars sell for twice the price of the average house it would take a German called Roland Gumpert to build something as ugly and uncompromising as the Apollo. This is a genuinely race-ready sports GT with styling led solely by aerodynamic necessity and fewer creature comforts than a night in the cells.

Its Audi-sourced, twin-turbo, 4.2-litre V8 can be tuned towards 800bhp but even in base spec the Apollo will pass 220mph. That brutish body provides so much downforce, meanwhile, that Gumpert has claimed his car can be driven upside-down on the roof of a tunnel. Although neither he, nor anyone else, is too eager to test the theory.

2005 **Toyota Aygo** ▶

When Toyota unveiled its joint project with Citroën and Peugeot their USP was price. The Aygo demonstrated an ingenious new way of cost-cutting, with simplicity and functionality becoming a stylish virtue rather than a crappy compromise. But the Aygo was also a blast to drive, with its low weight, skinny tyres and light, direct controls turning it into a modern-day Fiat 500. Before the actual modern-day Fiat 500 turned up and proved to be a bit shit.

2005 Citroën C6 ▶

Every so often Citroën launches a car that utterly baffles the buying public for about a decade before becoming a stone-cold classic. So it will be with the C6, a barge-like budget executive saloon replete with adventurous design ideas and a total disregard for market trends.

To sit inside the C6 is to be transported to another world. To put it in gear is to drive to that other world in a Valium-tinted cloud of Parisian chic. The steering is so light you think you're actually the passenger, the ride so supple you wonder if you have a terrible head cold. All timeless angles and economy of style, the C6 is high-end French motoring at its unique best.

2005 TVR Sagaris ▼

Just before TVR turned up its toes for the umpteenth time, it launched the Sagaris. Borrowing its name from an ancient battleaxe, this was nevertheless a rather modern product by Blackpool standards, with greater attention to detail and a superb, track-tuned chassis.

Still devoid of driver aids, even ones as ubiquitous as ABS, the 185mph Sagaris was a ferocious little beast that required total concentration to keep it on the straight and narrow. But this was promising stuff from a company that finally seemed to be finding its feet, just as the rug was pulled out from under it.

2005 **Ferrari 575 Superamerica** ▶

Keen to squeeze a little more life from its ageing 575 and a little more money out of its clientele, Ferrari unveiled the bizarre but beautiful Superamerica. Using an uprated version of its 5.7-litre V12, now with 540bhp and a top speed of 199mph, this was billed as the world's fastest convertible thanks to an ingenious glass-roof panel that hinged back through 180 degrees to lie across the boot.

This 'Revocromico' roof, electro-chromatic in something closer to layman's terms, could tint at the touch of a button from a normal glass translucency, through five stages to almost complete blackout. This allowed the driver to perfectly modulate not only brightness but also heat in the cabin, until time came to flip the whole thing open at the touch of another button.

The £191,000 Superamerica's flaw was that in doing so the interior of the panel then became the exterior, which got very dirty and then become the interior again. Expensive hair-dos ruined from Miami to Monte Carlo.

2005 **Maybach Exelero** ▼

The Mercedes-Benz Maybach limousine was a nightmarish vision of what happens when Too Much Money meets Not Enough Taste. And the Exelero showed how to undo the damage in one fell swoop, albeit with even more money and a touch of creative lunacy. Harking back to Maybach's own pre-war streamlining experiments in its retro-futuristic styling and using the 57 S limo's 700bhp, 6.0-litre, twin-turbo V12, the one-off, six-metre long, two-seat Exelero could sail past 200mph and see off 60mph in 4.4 seconds. None too shabby for a car weighing nearly 2.7 tonnes.

2005 **Suzuki Swift Sport** ▼

In an era of heavyweight hot-hatches, the majority of which the average spotty adolescent wouldn't be able to afford until he was cashing in his pension, Suzuki came to the rescue with the Swift Sport. This took the modest but attractive three-door Swift, and threw in a fettled 123bhp, 1.6-litre engine and stiffer suspension settings. Sensible trimmings like body-hugging seats and 17-inch alloys gave the Sport the look and feel it was after,

but it was an inherent low weight – a rare attribute by the mid-noughties – that provided an old-school hot hatch driving experience, where power was secondary to white-knuckle driver involvement.

Bags of grip, an addictive, free-revving powertrain and a price tag of just £11,500 made this the Mini Cooper for people without second homes and a paunch.

◄ 2005 **Corvette C6.R**

The racing car that breathed new life into Corvette for the new millennium, the C6.R was a hugely successful GT1 Le Mans veteran that spawned the Z06 and ZR1 road cars.

The focus, and usually the victor, of some truly epic tussles with Aston Martin's Prodrive DBR9, the C6.R was an unmistakable sight and sound through the long nights of international endurance racing. Its bright yellow livery crossed the line first at Le Mans in both 2005 and 2006 before Aston finally redressed the balance.

2006 **Toyota Hilux (North Pole Special)** ▲

Top Gear has made much of the indestructible nature of the Toyota Hilux, having failed to drown it, crash it, crush it or burn it. Small wonder, then, that Jeremy and James turned to their road-going Rasputin when bidding to be the first men to drive to the North Pole. Equipped with an essential survival kit comprising of some winches, big tyres and a bumper supply of gin and tonic, the pair set off in a very one-sided race against Richard Hammond on a dog sled.

Despite some genuinely grave scrapes and a few terse exchanges at the Hilux helm, the car and crew reached magnetic north in just under a week, the first motor vehicle in the history of everything to do so.

2006 Audi R10 V12 TDI ▼

Surgically removing the 'sport' from sports car racing, Audi debuted the R10 in 2006, a prototype endurance car that was incapable of losing. It won its inaugural race at Sebring in March and then took the chequered flag at the Le Mans 24 Hours for the next three years on the trot. The whole R10 project was a wildly expensive attempt to make diesel seem sexy, particularly to Americans, who had lost their taste for the stuff twenty-odd years beforehand. Audi's TDI diesel technology provided the ultimate blend of frugal, reliable power and torque, making it ideal for long distance racing. Diesel still wasn't sexy, of course, but you couldn't help fancying the R10.

2006 **Vauxhall Monaro** ▶

Rebranding GM Australia's muscular Monaro, Vauxhall found themselves with an unlikely hit on their hands in 2006. With a mighty 6.0-litre V8 thundering out 400bhp to the rear wheels in an unashamedly simple chassis, this was beefy, blokeish motoring at its meat-and-two-veg best. The Old Testament engineering of the Vauxhall Monaro did, however, have one saving virtue – it made the thing cheap. Nowhere else could you get that sort of grunt for less than £30k, although whatever savings you'd made usually went up in tyre smoke and unburned fuel.

2006 **Ferrari P4/5** ▼

There are a lot of very rich people out there who have no idea what to do when it comes to buying cars. How else do Bentley and Range Rover stay in business? Happily there are a few mega-wealthy petrolheads who know better, none more so than movie mogul Jim Glickenhaus. In 2006 he commissioned Ferrari to rebuild an Enzo – not exactly a bad car in the first place – in homage to the late-60s 330 racers. The result was simply astonishing. The P4/5 is a fully functioning 225mph supercar with the impossible styling of a show-stopping concept. And to his eternal credit, Jim drives his one-off, £2.5 million motor on the door handles whenever he can.

9 January 2006

DCI Gene Hunt becomes a national star for driving around in a Mark III Ford Cortina 2000E. The car is one of the stars of TV series Life On Mars, *when modern-day detective Sam Tyler is hurled through time to 1973 after being run over by a Vauxhall Cavalier.*

2006 **Ascari A10** ▲

For a long while, the A10 has perched high on *Top Gear*'s power-laps leader board. But so it should.

Designed as a road-legal racer that would garner more attention for Ascari's street projects, the A10 cost an eye-watering £350,000, and for that you didn't even get a stereo. But if you were able to hear anything over the sound of that 625bhp, 5.0-litre V8, uprated from its original employ in the BMW M5, it was only ever going to be the pounding of your terrified heart.

◀ 2006 **Ferrari 599 GTB**

When the 599 GTB Fiorano finally replaced the seemingly ancient 575 Maranello as Ferrari's front-engined, V12 flagship, it set a worrying precedent for the marque's major rivals like Aston Martin and Lamborghini. The old boys from Modena had seriously upped their game, creating a staggeringly high-tech, blisteringly quick, yet tractable and comparatively affordable sporting GT.

Born for another age with its aluminium spaceframe, magnetically adjustable dampers, auto box with 100 millisecond shifts and pointless, compelling launch control, this was the Ferrari of tomorrow, today. And more remarkable than anything was just how approachable a 200mph V12 Ferrari could now be.

2006 **Spyker C8 Laviolette** ▼

A sports car inspired by pre-war aviation and made by a Dutchman seems like an exceedingly risky way to invest £200k. But then you clap eyes on the Spyker C8 Laviolette and out comes the chequebook.

The compact C8 took its 400bhp from Audi's 4.2-litre V8, snugly mounted amidships inches behind the driver. With an extruded aluminium chassis and hand-beaten aluminium body panels, this retro-futuristic sculpture weighed just 1275kg, giving it a power-weight-ratio to match the wind-cheating styling.

The 'Laviolette' element is a panoramic glass roof that better shows off perhaps the most remarkable interior in modern motoring. Taking its inspiration from luxury aircraft cabins and, at a guess, Dan Dare comics, the cabin is a masterstroke of toggle switches, turned aluminium and quilted leather, giving it an air of atomic-age luxury.

The C8 fell far short of cheaper rivals in dynamic terms, but nothing this side of a Pagani Zonda has put so many jaws on the floor without even turning a wheel.

2006 **Koenigsegg CCX** ▶

The Koenigsegg CCX has a special place in *Top Gear*'s collective heart. Partly because it's a genuine 240mph hypercar that's been built in a Swedish shed, and partly because it's the one that almost saw off the Stig.

With its twin-supercharged V8 putting out in excess of 800bhp, this ultra-light, carbon-fibre bodied two-seater with its ultra-slippery aerodynamics and stumpy wheelbase needed to be treated with the sort of care and respect normally saved for diffusing bombs. After a spectacular, full-throttle visit to the tyre wall at the *Top Gear* track, the Stig recommended that Koenigsegg offer a rear spoiler to improve rear-end grip, which to this day they still do.

2006 **Porsche 997 GT3 RS** ▶

Continuing the lightweight lineage that began back in 1973, Porsche gave the RS treatment to its already pared-back and track-honed 997 GT3. The changes were subtle but vital: weight was reduced by 20kg via a plexiglass rear window and carbon-fibre spoiler, the wheelbase lengthened by 5mm to improve stability, the rear track widened by 44mm for greater grip. The already stiff suspension was turned up another notch and the on-board aids adjusted accordingly, while a lighter flywheel allowed for a freer-revving engine.

The real-world reality for the RS, nearly £15,000 more expensive than the standard GT3, was that it had improved imperceptibly to all but the expert racing driver. But this was the engineering apex of one of history's greatest sports cars. And you could have it in a unique shade of orange.

2006 **SSC Ultimate Aero** ▶

If you can't fully trust the Swedes when it comes to making a Bugatti Veyron rival, what are you meant to think when some west-coast Americans have a go? The SSC Ultimate Aero is not, in fact, a massive chocolate bar, but instead the unlikely, yet official, one-time fastest car in the world, with a top speed of 256mph. Using a supercharged, 6.3-litre V8, SSC managed to find a mind-boggling 1,187bhp and put it all through 20-inch rear wheels completely unassisted by traction control. They had to recruit a 71-year-old to do the high-speed runs, however, which says something about general confidence in the project.

2007 **Audi S5** ▶

The first decade of the new millennium saw Audi reinvented. No longer the conservative default for high-achieving, low-profile business types, it became a globally recognised status symbol. The A5, meanwhile, marked Audi's return to coupé production, with this one turning the humdrum and ubiquitous A4 saloon into a far more desirable and exclusive two-door. The S5 then threw in the grunt owners were clamouring for, with a 354bhp, 4.2-litre V8 from the RS4 whisking the nuclear Audi family to 60mph in 5.1 seconds. Serene, fast and just the right side of classy, the S5 is one of those rare cars that seems to have all bases covered.

2007 **Caparo T1** ▼

Every so often a car comes along that makes dubious claims about bringing Formula 1 technology and performance to the road. The Caparo cost close to a quarter of a million quid but was hugely underdeveloped and impractical. Almost undriveable at low speeds and with a tendency to catch fire at higher ones, this was not a car for the faint of heart. Nevertheless, a 470kg kerbweight and 575bhp output meant it had twice the power-to-weight ratio of a Bugatti Veyron and could hit 100mph in five seconds.

◄ 2007 **Fiat Panda 100hp**

At the opposite end of the performance spectrum to F1 cars with number plates is the Panda 100hp. You could buy 20 for the price of a single Caparo T1 and they'd all work every time, without catching fire.

The Panda 100hp exploited all the virtues of the standard car's low weight and low price, creating a bargain hot-hatch with its uprated engine, slammed and stiffened suspension and subtle but effective design tweaks. Not actually that quick but a hoot around town and affordable to buy, insure and run, the 100hp was to the real world what the Caparo was to teenage daydreams.

2007 **Nissan GTR** ▶

The big hoo-ha when Nissan launched the GTR was that it would be faster than a £90,000 Porsche 911 Turbo, but cost around half as much. After import it was near enough £60k, but proved quicker both to 60mph and over a flying lap of the Nordschleife, so in many respects it was 'job done.' Porsche grumbled about cheating with non-standard tyres, but the fact remained that the GTR significantly undercut its base-level 911 and out-performed its flagship. This was a technological tour de force that made up for anything it lacked in character with brutal, clinical ability. Supercar performance, going for a song.

2007 **Alfa Romeo 8C Competizione** ▼

Reminding a forgetful public that it still makes some the best-looking cars in the world, and makes them really quite badly, Alfa Romeo launched the 8C Competizione in 2007. A highly limited run of just 500 coupés and a further 500 soft-top versions were all sold unseen to very wealthy people unlikely to care if it turned out to be rubbish.

Using a 450bhp version of Maserati's own V8, shrouded in lightweight carbon-fibre bodywork, the £110,000 8C was quick, but only just. And it didn't handle.

But none of that mattered because it was then, and will surely always be, one of the most beautiful coupés of all time.

2007 **Mercedes-Benz CLK Black** ▶

To celebrate 40 years of tweaking sensible Mercs into performance leviathans, AMG took the underwhelming CLK coupé, gave it the customary course of steroids, then tightened the screw all over again with an array of brutal, race-inspired enhancements. The £100,000 CLK 63 AMG Black had turned a sea breeze into a cyclone.

Its 6.2-litre V8 was now putting 500bhp to the rear wheels, where a wider track with revised suspension settings sat beneath beefed up, bespoke and more aerodynamic bodywork. A stripped interior, trimmed in carbon fibre with bucket seats up front and none behind, completed the picture of total performance commitment. This was a six-figure CLK with the Porsche 911 GT3 squarely in its cross-hairs.

2007 **Aston Martin DBS** ▲

Despite immediate endorsement from the Bond franchise, the DBS was always going to be more Premiership bling than espionage in evening dress. This was a DB9 gone Goldie Lookin Chain, with most of the class lipo'd out and extra performance squirted in like so much collagen.

But this overlooks the fact that the DBS transformed the 9 from sedate GT into seriously capable supercar. Not quite a match for the more expensive Ferrari 599 GTB, this was nevertheless a fine replacement for the ageing Vanquish and a sure-fire money-spinner for the increasingly savvy Aston.

2007 **Suzuki XL7 Pikes Peak** ▼

Pikes Peak is an infamous 12-mile Colorado hill climb that has no rival this side of a wet Nordschleife for turning racing gods into thumb-sucking mortals. The finish line is 4300 metres above sea level, at which point cars will have lost up to thirty per cent of their power and many drivers are using breathing apparatus.

Suzuki employee Nobuhiro Tajima purpose-built his car around the firm's XL7 SUV, but threw in 1007bhp from a twin-turbo V6 engine and a rear wing of jumbo-jet proportions. The XL7 held the record for four years before it was smashed again. By Tajima, in another Suzuki. His nickname at work is Monster.

2007 **Bowler Wildcat** ▶

Using the Meccano kit that is a Land Rover Defender as its starting point, Midlands-based Bowler Offroad proceeded to create one of the quickest all-terrain vehicles of all time. The Wildcat was heavily bespoke, fitted with a variety of V8 petrol and turbo-diesel engines, making it ideal for any number of applications. Hugely successful on the Dakar rally, Wildcats have also been modified for secretive military use – the ultimate endorsement, if not the best product placement.

2007 **Lamborghini Gallardo Superleggera** ▼

The Gallardo first appeared in 2003, a smaller, more modern, more affordable and more useable alternative to the massive and expensive Murcielago. It immediately ran the risk of overshadowing Lamborghini's V12 flagship, all the more so in 2007 when the Superleggera, meaning 'super light', burst onto the scene in shades of orange and iridescent green.

The factory had managed to shave a considerable 100kg off the Gallardo's kerbweight with the extensive use of carbon fibre both inside and out. Unique magnesium wheels reduced unsprung weight at the Superleggera's corners, while carbon ceramic brakes increased its stopping power. The six-speed, e-gear transmission became standard, too, and an extra 9bhp was tweaked out of the engine. A fixed carbon rear wing, weighing next to nothing but adding a significant amount of high-speed downforce, completed a compelling little picture of raw and track-bent performance.

The results made a good car great, and the Superleggera went from being a curious alternative to the superior fare from Ferrari, to being the thinking man's choice in this heart-led corner of the car market. The gauntlet had been thrown squarely at Ferrari's feet...

2007 **Ferrari F430 Scuderia** ▼

Running in the sort of eerie parallel that smacks of industrial espionage, Ferrari's F430 appeared just after the Lamborghini Gallardo, and its lightened, hardened and more focussed version of this, the Scuderia, was unveiled just behind the Superleggera.

This was set to be the mother of all tussles, with the Scud also shaving 100kg from its kerbweight and increasing power to a fraction short of its Modenese neighbour.

What gave Ferrari the edge, however, was an extensive reworking of its electronic black magic, the most telling results of which were evident in the lightening-quick, semi-auto gearbox. Swapping cogs in a scarcely believable 60 milliseconds, the F430 Scuderia brought near-F1 shift speeds to a road-legal car, albeit one with no stereo, no carpet and not much in the way of soundproofing.

Both the Gallardo Superleggera and F430 Scuderia used subtle alterations to create huge improvements on cars that were astonishingly good in the first place. Fat fighting had become the latest weapon in the supercar arms race, and the two Italians now joined the 911 GT3 RS in a mighty scrap to be the most focussed and uncompromising road-legal race-car on sale.

2007 Mercedes-Benz C63 AMG Estate ▶

The only thing that makes owning a £50,000 super-saloon universally acceptable is turning it into an estate. No-one begrudges you a 449bhp 6.2-litre V8 that'll hit 60mph in 4.5 seconds so long as there's room enough in the boot for a couple of spaniels and a pushchair.

Merc's C63 AMG saloon is the aggressive statement of over-achievement, its estate sibling a commendable expression of patriarchal benevolence that just so happens to bounce off the limiter at 155mph. Tell that to the judge, anyhow.

2007 Peugeot 908 HDI ▼

Taking a leaf out of Audi's book, in 2007 European whipping boys Peugeot turned up at Le Mans with a diesel. The closed cockpit 908 HDI FAP looked fantastic and its 5.5-litre V12 oil burner was more powerful than even the dominant Audis.

After a couple of epic scraps with their German counterparts, Peugeot finally prevailed on home soil in 2009, the first time it had done so at the 24 Hours in 16 years. French diesel was a force to be reckoned with once again. Although reliability was traditionally dubious.

21 July 2007

Harry Potter and the Deathly Hallows *is published, the last in a series of books perhaps best remembered for attempting to convince the world that a Ford Anglia could fly.*

2007 **Donkervoort D8 GT** ▶

Another weird, expensive and epically quick sports car built in tiny numbers by the Dutch, the Donkervoort is a Caterham gone all German. Colin Chapman's original idea is strongly in evidence in the D8 GT, but reliable, powerful running gear is supplied by no-nonsense Audi.

The GT moniker also demands a roof and doors, all of which Donkervoort has made out of carbon fibre, keeping the final kerbweight down to just 650kg. Offset by the same 1.8-litre turbocharged engine that powered the Audi TT, here tuned to 266bhp, the D8 is as fast as you'd expect but even more expensive. Yours, after tax, for around £90,000.

2007 **Ferrari 612 Scaglietti Sessanta** ▼

The 612 Scaglietti is an underappreciated masterpiece from Ferrari, with its subtle styling, long-legged V12 and genuine four-seat configuration making it one of the more enduring and useable propositions Ferrari has dreamed up in its long lifetime. The most collectible of these is the highly limited Sessanta edition, built to celebrate the firm turning 60. Finished in two-tone paint jobs that echoed its highly bespoke post-war GTs and fitted with an F1 paddle-shift and electrochromatic glass roof similar to that of the 575 Superamerica, this was the ultimate, opulent blend of classic and cutting edge.

2007/2008 **Mazda Furai** ▶

Part real world racer, part futuristic fancy, Mazda's one-off Furai used a proven Le Mans Series chassis beneath experimental wind-cheating bodywork. Power was similarly real-cum-radical, with 450bhp generated by a rotary engine fuelled by eco-friendly bioethanol.

Mazda intended the Furai to blur the boundaries between its road and racing projects, hinting at future design and tech directions. Instead it just made us forget that Mazda ever made anything else.

2008 **Lamborghini Estoque** ▶

The subject of much 'will they, won't they?' speculation from the off, the four-door Estoque was unveiled by Lamborghini as a 'possible' before an uncertain economic outlook turned it into a 'not on your life'.

But with its own profits soaring and the mega-saloon market now replete with Maseratis, Mercs, Aston Martins and Porsches, the possibility of this Espada revival becoming a production reality has never really seemed that far-fetched.

Powered by a 5.2-litre V10, mounted up front to make room in the rear for a proper row of seats, the Estoque would be as practical as it is fast and beautiful, the perfect supercar for a global recession.

2008 **Tesla Roadster** ▶

With emissions regulations and oil prices tightening their stranglehold on the sports car, the likes of the Tesla Roadster offer us all a ray of hope. This is the world's first full-electric performance car, based loosely on the Lotus Elise but rebodied and powered by lithium ion batteries and a 248bhp electric motor.

Noble environmental sensitivity notwithstanding, the principal advantage of this technology is that power through the Tesla's single gear is immediate. Press the fast pedal and wallop, you're gone in a near-silent swoosh of rev-free, exhaust-free, instantaneous acceleration. Green is for go.

◄ 2008 **Audi RS6 Avant**

If you had to own just one car for the rest of your life, you'd not regret a single day of it in the RS6 Avant. With supercar performance from its Lambo-sourced, 572bhp, twin-turbo, 5.0-litre V10, Audi's all-encompassing, all-wheel drive estate is spacious, comfortable, practical and reliable whilst managing to be biblically fast in any given situation. The only criticism ever levelled at the RS6 is that it makes going this quickly seem strangely uneventful. Can a car be too good?

22 July 2008

Ford celebrates a major landmark in automotive history, as 100 years have passed since the Model T first went into production.

2008 **Rolls-Royce Phantom Coupé** ▲

It's an odd idea, taking the Phantom limousine and removing a pair of doors. That a 2.6 tonne car might be considered sporty is optimistic to say the least, but when you have a 453bhp, 6.7-litre V12 to hand that can generate 531 lb ft of torque at just 3500rpm, you can afford to have a bit of optimism.

The Rolls-Royce Phantom Coupé is a 5.6-metre long, 2-metre wide stroke of plutocratic lunacy that will hit 60mph in 5.6 seconds and only stop at a restricted 155mph because braking hard from any faster would knock the planet off its axis. Yours for a snip at £300,000.

2008 **Fiat 500 Abarth** ▶

The bog-standard Fiat 500 was a bit of a disappointment to drive, with lifeless steering and a crappy driving position. The Abarth didn't redress these problems so much as mask them in a thrilling little package of design and dynamic enhancements. Looking ferocious with its gaping air dams, roof spoiler and optional 17-inch rims, and wringing 135bhp from its turbocharged 1.4-litre engine, the stiffer, lower 500 Abarth had become a brutal, beautiful thug of a thing.

2008 **Nissan 370 Z** ▶

Nissan's mid-market muscle car is one of the unsung heroes of modern motoring. For well under £30,000 you get a beefy, characterful, challenging and utterly reliable sports car that sets you apart from the default German rivals that all those estate agents and tennis coaches are buying up in droves. With 326bhp on offer through a meaty, manual gearbox, the 370Z will see off 60mph in five seconds and hit the limiter at 155mph. And it looks like a mini GTR.

◀ 2008 **VW Golf R32**

The R32 was always going to struggle to make a case for itself when the cheaper and comparably quick GTI was already being hailed as the best hot-hatch on sale. But with its four-wheel drive and bellicose 246bhp, 3.2-litre V6, there was a sense of drama to the R32 that you just couldn't find in any other car with rear seats and a proper hatchback boot. This was heart-over-head stuff, an expensive leave of your senses that you would never, ever regret.

2008 **Caterham R500** ▶

Continuous, fastidious evolution has brought Caterham's flagship R500 to a dizzying place. With 263bhp available in a car that weighs 506kg, this £37k pocket racer now has a greater power-to-weight ratio than the Bugatti Veyron. Lightened chassis with thinner aluminium panels and carbon fibre everywhere, sold for the first time with an optional sequential racing box and launch control, the R500's real virtue remains its simplicity. This is lightweight, high-power performance in the raw, often emulated, never bettered.

2008 **Dodge Challenger** ▼

Plundering its heritage in a tardy bid to get on the retro bandwagon, Dodge gave new life to its Challenger muscle car in late 2007. In the blink of an eye the entire '08 allocation had been snapped up – Mustang? What Mustang?

The Challenger's 425bhp, 6.1-litre Hemi V8 gives it huge dollops of lazy power and torque, offering unrivalled bangs for buck. But only in a straight line. Europeans need not apply.

2008 **KTM X-Bow** ▼

As the acknowledged experts in off-road motorcycles, KTM's announcement that it was about to build a pricey, high-tech track car raised a few eyebrows in the motoring press. But the fact that they were teaming up with both Audi and Italian chassis gurus Dallara quickly turned scepticism into feverish anticipation. The X-Bow features a massively strong, but light, carbon-fibre tub, in the middle of which sits Audi's 1.8-litre turbo, tuned to 237bhp. The driver sits before and beneath this, in a Blade Runner world of bare carbon and blinking LEDs.

On the move, the X-Bow demands and rewards respect in equal measure. With no computer trickery to flatter the novice, KTM's £45,000 black and orange bathtub is as fast as your skills and/or balls dare to make it.

2008 **Bentley Brooklands** ▶

Reacting to Rolls-Royce's Phantom Coupé, Bentley decided to take the angle grinder to its Arnage limousine. The resulting Brooklands was a mighty, pillarless, two-door GT, with a 6.75-litre, twin-turbo V8 making 530bhp, yours for a list price of £240,000 basic. The optional carbon ceramic brakes, something you justifiably might want on a car weighing nearly three tonnes, would set you back another £20k.

Huge in the sense normally reserved for ocean-going cargo vessels, impossibly fast in spite of this and exactly as expensive as all this engineering, polishing and hand-stitching of ex-cows would suggest, the Brooklands was a palatial point-and-squirt coupé of the old school. Only 550 were ever made, all of them sold unseen.

2008 Aston Martin Vantage V12 ▼

The one thing the Aston Martin V8 Vantage always lacked was sufficient poke to make a superb driving experience truly extraordinary. But shoehorn beneath that stubby bonnet the 510bhp, 6.0-litre V12 from the flagship DBS and, safe to say, problem solved.

The V12 Vantage is one of Aston's all-time greats, with the class and refinement owners have come to expect from Britain's most iconic motoring brand now deftly combined with an astonishing and addictive turn of speed.

Apart from a price tag of £135,000 – and this still significantly undercuts the DBS – there simply is no fault to be found in Aston's hybrid supercar-cum-GT. It covers all the performance bases, and does so with a character and style that is unsurpassed at twice the price.

2008 **Audi R8 V10** ▶

The 911-bashing Audi R8 was one of those rare cars that exceeded its own hype. The perfect cocktail of class, comfort, performance and usability, it seemed impossible to improve upon. Until, inevitably, Audi threw in a couple more cylinders, making its Teutonic masterpiece a direct rival for the Lamborghini Gallardo in the full-bore supercar market.

The R8 V10 deftly balanced understatement and ferocious grunt, with its compact, 5.2-litre, 10-cylinder tuned to 518bhp. In every respect an improvement over the V8, and for not that much more money, the R8 V10 put its junior sibling to the sword.

2008 **Lamborghini Reventon** ▶

Apparently impressed by recent US foreign policy, Lamborghini decided to rebuild its Murcielago to stealth bomber specifications. Only 20 Reventons were ever made, which was sensible considering they cost a million Euros before tax and were no faster than the standard LP-640 on which they were based.

But this was haute couture for the highway, with both exterior and interior radically redesigned in muted tones and aggressive, purposeful angles. A bonkers indulgence undoubtedly, but the catwalk dictates the high street.

2008 **Ginetta G50** ▶

The G50 marked the moment when Ginetta, yet another low-volume British sports car manufacturer with Big Dipper fortunes, began its convincing and thoroughly modern revival. Designed in-house and powered by a 300bhp 3.5-litre Ford V6, the G50 was essentially a single-make racer with a rough-and-ready road-going option. Competition-ready chassis dynamics and a kerbweight of just 950kg provided straight-line speed and B-road handling to rival cars costing three times as much.

2008 GTbyCitroën ▼

Originally designed for a virtual, promotional existence, the GTbyCitroën caused such a furore that the PSA powers-that-be put it into production as a one-off driveable concept. A wild and improbable beast, even by Citroën's reliably insane standards, it was almost impossible to see out of, noisier than the hounds of hell and worth millions, in part due to the extraordinary polished copper interior.

2008 Mercedes-Benz SL63 AMG ▶

The elegant and rapid SL coupé/cabriolet probably never really needed the AMG treatment but, once done, there was no looking back. The original supercharged SL55 was an engine with a car attached. The SL63, with its 518bhp of naturally aspirated 6.2-litre V8, was the complete package. With long-legged cruising ability now seamlessly mated to genuine sporting composure, this was a fascinating and multi-faceted sports tourer. The only catch was the £100k sticker price.

2009 **Pagani Zonda Cinque Roadster** ▶

After a decade of glacially slow but peerlessly fastidious production, the Zonda had run its course. To celebrate, Pagani built a final five Roadsters, using a retuned version of its Mercedes-Benz AMG-sourced, 7.3-litre V12, now pushing out 669bhp via a six-speed sequential gearbox. Lower and stiffer thanks to the extensive use of titanium-reinforced carbon fibre, the £1.1million Zonda Cinque Roadster was a fitting, and aptly expensive, send-off for one of the world's all-time great supercars.

◀ 2009 **Radical SR8**

To the ire of all sorts, particularly Porsche, the Radical SR8 continues to claim lap after fastest lap at the Nordschleife for a car designated as road legal. And although it wouldn't look out of place on the starting grid at Le Mans, nor sound it with its twin superbike powerplant revving to 10,000rpm, the SR8 really will take you to Tesco if you want it to.

2009 **Mini Cooper S** ▶

Blessed with a superb chassis and direct, informative steering, the Mini Cooper S is the other great hot-hatch to consider when toying with the idea of a Renaultsport Clio. With 181bhp squeezed from its turbocharged, 1.6-litre BMW unit, there's plenty of poke offset by even better running costs. Although not quite as dynamically involving as its cheese-eating chum, the slightly pricier Mini is more about class and refinement, making this the go-to performance car for the middle-aged urbanite with a little lead left in his pencil.

2009 **Brawn BGP 001** ▼

Of all the modern championship-winning F1 cars that could have graced these pages, the Brawn BGP 001 takes the limelight for debuting in such romantic fashion. Having bought out a failing Honda F1 package, Ross Brawn united his car with a Mercedes-Benz engine and Jenson Button, who guided it to both Drivers and Constructor's titles. Job done, Brawn sold on to Mercedes-Benz.

2009 **Citroën DS3** ▶

A curious blend of sporting intent with traditional Citroën style and flair, the DS3 was launched as a warm hatch that offered a sort of bespoke tailoring service in lieu of outright performance. The upshot was undeniably brilliant. Instead of tarting up an existing model, Citroën had created something entirely new and rather special which it then encouraged you to make unique. The DS3 brings personalisation to an increasingly impersonal industry.

2009 Audi E-Tron ▶

The world in 2009 was quite sated by the R8 in its various guises, but Audi wasn't done. The E-Tron is its mesmerising vision for our all-electric performance future, but one that the firm intends to sell in limited numbers. Clearly based on the R8, but in truth shorter and lower, the E-Tron has an electric motor driving each wheel, making 313bhp and over 3,000lb ft of torque. This means ballistic levels of silent acceleration, rivalled only by the Tesla Roadster. Our motoring tomorrow may be uncertain, but it's got a lot of promise.

2009 Zenvo ST1 ▼

Destined for an obscurity it doesn't deserve, the Danish-designed Zenvo ST1 was a 1,100bhp hypercar that looked like a paper dart, if paper darts were all made by the Stig. With a top speed limited to 233mph from its supercharged and turbocharged, 7.0-litre V8, outright performance was right up there with the Veyrons and Koenigseggs of this world. So how could a car like this drop so comprehensively off the radar? It might have something to do with the £700,000 price tag, or the fact that only 15 will ever be made.

8 Jan 2009

Further proof, were it needed, that money doesn't buy good sense, as footballer Cristiano Ronaldo crashes and writes off his £200,000 Ferrari 599 GTO in a tunnel on the outskirts of Manchester.

◄ 2009 **Renaultsport Clio 200 Cup**

The 21st-century car is expanding in every direction, in terms of weight, of size and of price. Left to remind us what might have been are hen's teeth rarities like the Clio Cup. Costing less than £16,000, weighing just over 1200kg and small enough to position properly in a fast, tightening corner, Renault's inspirational hot-hatch is, pound-for-pound, the best performance car on sale. With supple but focussed suspension, an eager 197bhp normally aspirated engine and responsive, organic controls, this is a true driver's car in the old-world sense. No microchip interference, no space-age substitutes for engineering excellence. As good as it gets, as cheap as it comes.

2009 **Pagani Zonda R** ▼

In the vein of the Ferrari FXX, Pagani did one last thing with the Zonda, and that was build an 'R' version that was neither eligible for competition nor road legal. The all-black, all-carbon R, a smorgasbord of wind-cheating wings and spoilers, was a test bed for future technologies, enabling the tiny Modenese company to prove developments for the Zonda's then top-secret replacement.

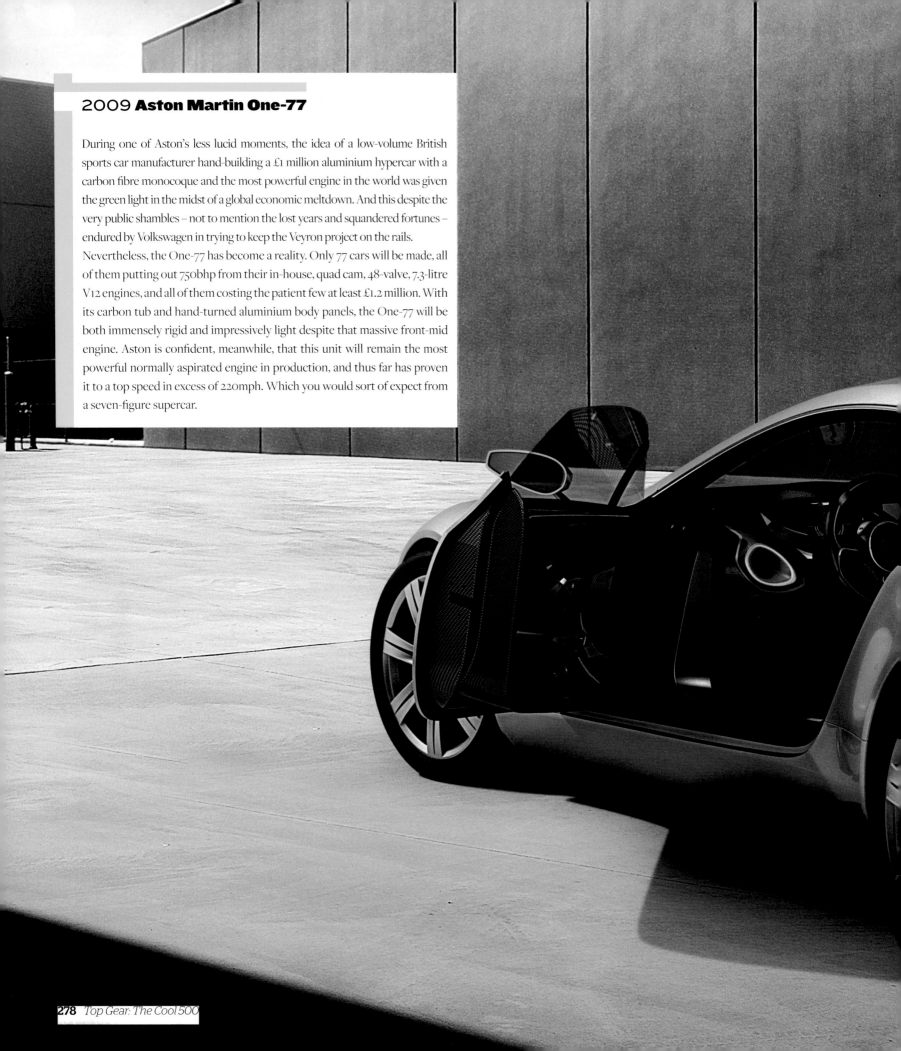

2009 Aston Martin One-77

During one of Aston's less lucid moments, the idea of a low-volume British sports car manufacturer hand-building a £1 million aluminium hypercar with a carbon fibre monocoque and the most powerful engine in the world was given the green light in the midst of a global economic meltdown. And this despite the very public shambles – not to mention the lost years and squandered fortunes – endured by Volkswagen in trying to keep the Veyron project on the rails. Nevertheless, the One-77 has become a reality. Only 77 cars will be made, all of them putting out 750bhp from their in-house, quad cam, 48-valve, 7.3-litre V12 engines, and all of them costing the patient few at least £1.2 million. With its carbon tub and hand-turned aluminium body panels, the One-77 will be both immensely rigid and impressively light despite that massive front-mid engine. Aston is confident, meanwhile, that this unit will remain the most powerful normally aspirated engine in production, and thus far has proven it to a top speed in excess of 220mph. Which you would sort of expect from a seven-figure supercar.

2009 **Lamborghini Concept S** ▼

The Gallardo–based, twin-cockpit Concept S was created by Lamborghini's head of design, Luc Donckerwolke, who borrowed inspiration from bygone single-seater racing cars and, quite possibly, an argument with his wife. Improving both aerodynamics and engine cooling by channelling air between driver and passenger, and from there directly into the engine, the Concept S was a beautiful and highly logical, if slightly antisocial, solution to the supercar designer's perennial problem.

2009 **Veritas RS3** ▶

The Veritas RS3 is yet another quarter-of-a-million-quid crackpot attempt to make a 200mph supercar in a shed, albeit a German shed this time, doubtless spotlessly clean and with its own electricity supply. Power comes from the latest BMW M3's superb V8, tuned here to 473bhp, and in a car that weighs a little over a tonne, that's enough to make the maker's claims of a 200mph top speed almost plausible. If unappealing, what with it not having a windscreen. Or ABS brakes.

2009 **Volkswagen Scirocco** ▶

Seemingly blessed with a Midas' touch for motoring, Volkswagen took an inspired gamble in 2009 when it breathed new life into the long-dead Scirocco. Based on the Golf platform, but lower, wider and with outrageous coupé styling, it trod an artful line between VW's traditional understatement and the rakish lines of the head-turning concept that previewed it.

A practical, proper four-seater with engines ranging from frugal diesels to turbo-charged, white-knuckle petrols, the Scirocco did – and still does – dependable and desirable in equal measure. The last thing that could make that claim was, predictably, the Golf GTI.

2009 **Noble M600** ▼

Against a tidal wave of new supercars from all the major international players, plucky little Noble fired up its M600 in 2009. With a 650bhp, twin-turbo V8 working against just 1250kg of kerbweight, the involving and communicative M600 hit 60mph in 3.0 seconds and claimed a theoretical top speed of 225mph. The catch was the price tag: £200k was more than the latest wares from Ferrari and McLaren and for that you didn't even get ABS brakes. Lunacy then, but the gloriously compelling sort that tiptoes into genius.

20 January 2009

George W. Bush waits on the White House steps as the Presidential State Car, a custom-built limo known as 'Cadillac One', delivers the building's new tenant – President Barack Obama. Along with the White House door keys, President Obama receives the keys to an all-new, $300,000 Cadillac One.

2009 **Chevrolet Corvette ZR1** ▶

Finally able to go round corners and offering an unrivalled ratio of power-to-pound sterling, the historically maligned Corvette experienced a renaissance in the 21st century. And the epitome of this was the 638bhp ZR1. This ultimate evolution of the C6 range was equipped with far more sophisticated suspension and a massive supercharger that barrelled it to 100mph in just seven seconds and on to a top speed of 205mph.

◀ 2009 **Renaultsport Megane R26.R**

The final, final refinement of Renault's GTI rival, the R26.R took up where the R26 F1 left off, using its superb chassis, teeth-rattling suspension and eager turbo, but shedding a massive 123kg of weight via polycarbonate windows, carbon-fibre bonnet, no rear seats and almost no soundproofing. With rollcage and red racing alloys thrown in, this was now an uncompromising track day tool and the fastest front-wheel drive car to lap the Nordschleife.

2009 **Audi TT RS** ▶

The new TT, bereft of its predecessor's design flair, was nevertheless a vastly more accomplished piece of engineering, ripe for an RS overhaul. Now with wider track, four-wheel drive as standard and an all-new 335bhp, 2.5-litre, 5-cylinder, turbocharged engine that evoked the sonorous powerplant from the original Quattro, this was an emotional experience closer to the flagship R8 than its £42k price tag should have allowed.

2009 **BMW VED** ▼

An acronym for Vision Efficient Dynamics, the one-off VED concept was BMW's way of explaining its design direction. Managing M3 performance with Mini fuel economy thanks to a plug-in turbodiesel hybrid, and all in the latest lightweight and light-enhancing four-seat coupé package, this is the future of motoring if we're all very, very lucky indeed. In truth, we'll probably just be getting the bus.

2009 **Porsche Panamera Turbo** ▶

When the Panamera first appeared in 2009, everyone got hung up on how horrendously ugly it was. And quite right, too. So Porsche hurried out the £100k, 493bhp Turbo, a four-wheel drive, twin-turbocharged V8 variant that would hit 60mph in just over four seconds and top out at 188mph. Not bad for a two-tonne, four-seat executive saloon with a 432-litre boot. Hugely fast and horribly expensive, suddenly styling was the least of your worries.

2009 **Bentley Continental Supersports** ▼

Six years old and showing it, Bentley put its Continental GT on a crash diet. The bods behind the £163,000 Supersports shaved a significant 110kg off the previous performance flagship, the Speed, while fine-tuning its twin-turbo W12 engine to 621bhp and halving the time it takes to change gear.

With a rear-wheel bias now in the four-wheel drive system, much stiffer suspension and the liberal deployment of lightweight carbon fibre, the Supersports – still tipping the scales at 2.2 tonnes – was vastly more agile, could hit 204mph and see off 60mph in 3.7 seconds.

◄ 2009 **Ferrari 458**

Perhaps the greatest single endorsement of the 458 was made by McLaren. Poised at last to launch their overdue MP4-12C supercar, the Surrey-based F1 experts went back to the bunker for another major rethink after seeing Ferrari's mid-engined marvel for the first time.

A dizzying cocktail of high-tech wizardry and unfettered engineering genius, the 202mph 458, with its 562bhp V8 hollering from within one of the most effective cohesions of form and function in any area of design today, is as capable as it is desirable. Which is to say, almost without rival.

2009 **VW Bluesport** ▶

Continuing to tread that delicate line between the sensible, dependable Volkswagen of old and a recent upsurge in performance kudos, the Wolfsburg design team unveiled the oxymoronic Bluesport: an affordable, environmentally sensitive, mid-engined roadster. Powered by a 2.0-litre diesel engine, VW's mini Porsche Boxster can hit 60mph in under seven seconds and run on to 140mph. But all the while it is capable of returning a noble 50mpg.

Although only seen in concept form thus far, the Bluesport looks likely to become a production reality in the very near future. Fingers crossed.

2009 **Morgan Aeromax** ▼

Originally built as a one-off for a wealthy Swiss banker, the Aeromax caused such a clamour at the Geneva Motor Show that Morgan was pressured into building a single run of just 100 of these glorious Art Deco-inspired GTs. With BMW's 362bhp, 4.8-litre V8 tasked with whisking a remarkably modest 1180kgs of Aeromax to 60mph in 4.2 seconds and on to 170mph, there was a turn of speed to match the pre-war comic book looks. Priced at £110,000, all were sold before the factory had even got the kettle on.

2010s
THE PRESENT TENSE

uch is the rate of development in the world of cars that the start of this millennium feels far more distant than a mere decade. And now, as we enter the 21st-century's adolescence, its hormones are raging. Everywhere there is growth and change, investment and improvement, with new highs in power output and top speeds, but also in miles to the ever more pricey gallon, in safety and refinement. The ultimate goal of any supercar designer, however, is no longer simple. With ever-increasing performance must come reduced emissions, greater sustainability, a semblance of social responsibility in a once gleefully carefree industry.

Around the world, meanwhile, chaos ensues with metronomic reliability. Team America is spiking the price of crude to unprecedented levels as it wages both noisy and silent wars in the oil-rich Middle East. The 'Green' agenda is now universal, with every stab of the throttle necessarily accompanied by a lash from the mental birch.

Historians will doubtless reflect on the 'Twenty-Tens' as the decade of financial crises, with double-dip recessions and the collapse of the Euro bankrupting entire countries and causing the once mighty auto industry to recede into a new epoch of caution and efficiency.

But as the fortunes of one continent plummet, so they soar on another, and the low-volume, high-price end of the car market could not be in ruder health. We read in magazines we can't afford, over the shoulders of fellow public transport-ees, about ever more exotic four-wheeled fare. In the worst financial doldrums since the Wall Street Crash of the 1920s there are newer, faster, even more expensive supercars from Lamborghini, Ferrari, Pagani and McLaren to name but a few. Iran is building the bomb, Israel digging some shelters and all the while the high-performance cottage industry ploughs on regardless in the shadow of total annihilation. For which we will be grateful long after the mushroom clouds have settled.

2010 **Jaguar XJ Supersport** ▶

It took the best part of half a century, but when Jaguar finally reinvented the XJ they did a sterling job of it. Deftly balancing limo-like refinement with that vital element of sporting DNA that even the biggest Jag has to have, the XJ – especially when equipped with the Supersport's 503bhp supercharged 5.0-litre V8 – was instantly mixing it with the big boys from Audi, BMW and Mercedes-Benz.

Its all-aluminium construction helps match a remarkable turn of speed with tolerable economy, but its stunning styling, both inside and out, is what separates it from the ubiquitous German heavyweights.

2010 **Lexus LFA** ▼

After what felt like a lifetime of waiting, with endless teasers and delays and spy shots and more delays, the Lexus LFA finally emerged in 2010. And it was every bit as astonishing as all those years and all those yen promised it would be.

Aside from the intergalactic styling, all of which is wind-tunnel work rather than designer's whimsy, the LFA boasts one of the most emotive and able engines ever to have graced a road car. This 552bhp, 4.8-litre V10 can rev to 9,000rpm in less than a second, so fast, its makers state, that a physical needle can't keep up. And the digital one will indicate a top speed of 202mph, with 60mph despatched in 3.7 seconds.

Only 500 LFAs were made, each of them sold ahead of production for a toe-curling £340,000.

2010 **Murray T25** ▼

When the designer of the legendary McLaren F1 turned his hand to urban transport solutions, people were expecting magic. And they weren't disappointed. The 660cc, rear-engined T25 uses Formula 1 technology to create an immensely strong cell in which three occupants can sit in total comfort, the driver forward and central, with each passenger slightly farther back. This design, along with a single, forward-opening door, allows the T25 to be just 1.3 metres wide, meaning three of them can park side-by-side in the space one average car would occupy lengthways.

2010 **Honda CRZ** ▶

Slightly more in step with the times than Lexus, if not with the *Top Gear* id, Honda brought its eagerly anticipated CRZ to market in 2010. Billed as the first sporting hybrid, in truth it wasn't remotely fast and nor was it more economical than a decent diesel. But what the CRZ did do was give us a peep into the future, where cars will be cleaner without forgoing every last vestige of cool. The CRZ looks the business, handles like a true hot-hatch and might, one day, be hailed as the godfather of geek-free green motoring.

2010 **Porsche 918** ▶

In the 918 Porsche has, in theory, cracked it. Here is a 718bhp hypercar that, courtesy of its petrol/electric hybrid drivetrain, will hit 60mph in three seconds, pass 200mph, yet still be capable of returning 94mpg.

With a wary eye on survival in an uncertain market for thirsty performance cars, Porsche has chucked the kitchen sink at the 918 – the carbon monocoque from the Carrera GT; a race-bred V8 at the rear; three electric motors, two at the front wheels; and super-slippery aerodynamics that pay homage to past Porsche glories like the 917 and 718 RSK Spyder.

The 918 also features a regenerative braking system that will unleash an extra 200bhp at the touch of a button, giving it Formula 1-style overtaking abilities.

The catch, of course, is that at the moment such efforts in engineering will set you back well in excess of half a million quid. The order books are open however, with production slated for early 2013.

2010 **Maserati Grancabrio** ▼

The strict rules of physics have made the sporty, four-seat cabriolet something of an engineering Holy Grail, but Maserati's Grancabrio may, at long last, have completed the quest. Ahead of the driver is a 440bhp, 4.7-litre V8, good for 175mph and 0–60mph in 5.4 seconds, while behind him is a useable set of rear seats. Devoid of the usual shakes and rattles that plague large soft-tops, the Grancabrio is involving, rapid and luxurious. Its only flaw is a miniscule boot, not great in a four-up GT, especially one that's nearly five-metres long.

2010 **Ariel Atom 500** ▼

The Atom was already a lunatic proposition: no doors, roof, windscreen, not even a body panel, but a screaming Honda V-Tec engine mounted directly to the chassis just behind your head. The one thing this featherweight, 550kg adrenaline injection didn't need was a race-derived sequential gearbox coupled to a 500bhp 3.0 V8 that revs to 10,600rpm. You know what happened next. The Atom 500 lays convincing claim to being the fastest accelerating production car on Planet Earth. It'll hit 60mph in just 2.3 seconds and reach the ton in a further three. What's even more remarkable is that this single-seat racer's speed is utterly accessible, making the 500 entirely useable, if completely terrifying, on the public road. Perhaps wisely, Ariel decided to build just 25 examples, and despite a whopping pre-tax price tag of £125,000, they got snapped up.

2010 **Mercedes-Benz SLS AMG** ▼

Eschewing the light and nimble supercar mainstream, Merc's SLS is a large, comfortable grand tourer with the straight-line speed (and the price tag) of its most exotic rivals from Ferrari and Lamborghini. But what the SLS lacks in agility it more than makes up for in poise and presence, in no small part thanks to its iconic gull-wing doors.

Borrowing heavily from the original mid-50s 300SL Gull-wing, but without cynically plundering that priceless heritage in the process, the SLS is a glorious mash-up of old and new, with an all-aluminium chassis and hand-built, 563bhp, 6.2-litre V8 beneath a superbly crafted aluminium body that references past and present in skilful harmony.

The SLS will set you back £170,000 give or take, and for that you have far less of a sports car than the on-money rivals from Ferrari like the 599 GTB and 458 Italia. But this is stately stuff, moving in a different world from the playboy's default Italian fair. And still moving at one hell of a lick.

2010 Peugeot RCZ ▶

No-one seriously thought Peugeot would ever build the RCZ when it unveiled the original concept in 2007. This was Peugeot, after all, purveyors of the 308 and 207 SW, two of the least exciting cars in the world. But, three years on, it appeared right enough, looking remarkably similar to the implausibly beautiful show car, with its curvaceous glass rear screen and big cat stance.

Although not quite a dynamic rival for the Audi TT, there is nevertheless nothing else at this end of the market that is such a magnet for unabashed admiration. The RCZ isn't a great car, but it's a Peugeot that comes close, and that makes it really quite special.

2010 Aston Martin Rapide ▼

Keeping up with the Joneses, in this case the Italian and German Joneses at Maserati and Porsche, Aston Martin finally brought its oft-mooted, four-door DB9 to market in early 2010. The Rapide features the same excellent, 6.0-litre V12 as its two-door GT sibling, with 470bhp making this one of the fastest saloons on sale. Styling four doors into a convincingly sporty profile is a headache that has undone many a manufacturer, but Aston has it nailed with the Rapide. It's also managed to maintain that thoroughbred DNA, with a fantastic blend of agility and composure making this as impressive a sporting drive as it is a refined distance cruiser. Supercar status for the family man then, although said family man needs to find £140,000.

Reviving a 60s racing legend, the Chevron GR8 harks back to its beautiful, purposeful forebears while adding modern mechanicals and better aerodynamic understanding.

Sadly, it's not for sale in road-legal form, but anyone who fancies slaying a few Ferraris in the British GT championship need only find £50k for this Cosworth-powered, mid-engined track tool. In the world of privateer racing that's almost giving it away.

2010 **Audi RS3** ►

Although insanely expensive for what is, in the end, only a hot-hatch, the £40,000 Audi RS3 is still a truly formidable beast. Using the 2.5-litre, 5-cylinder unit from the TT RS, with massive traction guaranteed by Quattro four-wheel drive, the practical, almost understated, RS3 goes all Jekyll to Hyde in the blink of an eye, with its 335bhp seeing off 60mph in just 4.6 seconds.

◄ 2010 **BMW M3 GT2 Art Car**

Reviving an on/off tradition of getting immensely famous artists to design its racing liveries, in 2010 BMW gave its M3 GT2 Le Mans entrant to kitsch porn/art icon Jeff Koons. The results were extraordinary, but in a surprisingly good, family-friendly way. Reflecting the violent energy of race speeds, Koons applied vivid vinyl strips along the car's length, ending in an apposite collage of exploding debris: the car lasted less than six hours.

2010 **Lotus Evora** ▼

After years of rumour and insider gossip, 'Project Eagle' finally made it to the road. The Evora was Lotus' first grown-up car since the Esprit, and it had the price tag to match. Would anyone buy a £60,000 plastic car glued together in darkest Norfolk when they could have a Porsche Cayman S for less? When it handled this well, rode this serenely and looked like a shrink-wrapped supercar, the answer was an emphatic yes.

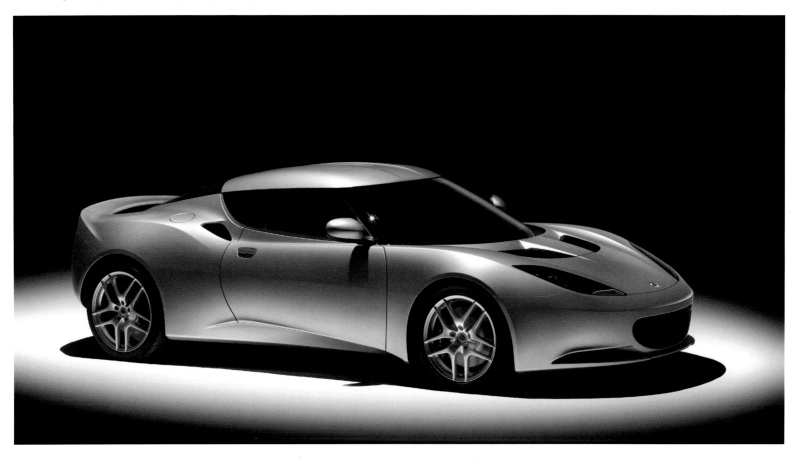

2010 **Bugatti Veyron SuperSport** ▶

The amount of column inches dedicated to the Bugatti Veyron probably equates quite nicely with the number of miles of tarmac this 1000bhp, quad-turbo, W16 supercar ate up in its years and years of warp speed testing. And yet, within a matter of months of its launch, this 253mph car-to-end-all-cars was no longer the fastest thing on earth, having been upstaged by the SSC Ultimate Aero.

It's easy to imagine the ructions in those Wolfsburg boardrooms when it was discovered that something not unlike the combined national debt of sub-Saharan Africa had been spent on a car that was already old news.

Enter, schnell-schnell, the Veyron SuperSport. With larger turbos and intercoolers adding another 196bhp, a reduction in weight thanks to even more carbon fibre, and lower, stiffer suspension to improve high-speed stability, the SuperSport was run at a simply inconceivable 267.91mph, making it again the fastest car in the world, and by rather a substantial margin. Order was restored in the Universe According to Volkswagen.

2011 **McLaren MP4-12C**

Causing almost as much of a stir as the Bugatti Veryron, and taking almost as long to turn up, the feverishly anticipated McLaren MP4-12C finally left the firm's high-tech Woking HQ in the summer of 2011.

A panoply of cutting-edge materials, ingenious design and blue-chip electronic industry, this was a direct rival to the incredible Ferrari 458, with comparable power, speed and price.

Unfortunately for McLaren, the near-universal collective opinion has come down on the side of the 458, principally because there is bowel-churning drama going spare in the Ferrari where the McLaren is a bit more like an episode of Open University.

That said, the biblically quick MP4-12C, with its carbon-fibre tub, hydraulic damping, ultra-efficient, 592bhp, twin-turbo V8 and seven-speed sequential gearbox, must be championed as a technological tour de force, however much it lacks a goosebump factor. This is clinical brilliance, worth the wait, and full of promise for McLaren's road-going future.

2011 BMW Z4 ▼

Having been derided as more than a little effeminate in its first incarnation, and heavily criticised for its 'flame surface' styling in the second, it was third time lucky for BMW with the Z3. Now with a folding hard top, cleaner styling and a vastly improved ride, this was the Porsche Boxster rival we'd all been waiting for. Almost. Its straight-six engines were predictably superb, but it's the expectation of an M-Sport version that keeps *Top Gear* on a steady simmer.

2011 Volvo C30 Polestar ▶

The C30 coupé/hatchback/whatever was a sales catastrophe for Volvo, who wanted to sell boat-loads of high-spec, sporty versions to hip, rich 20-somethings but could only attract silver-haired retirees downsizing from their entry-level S40s. So, in a (fairly desperate) bid to finally get Europe's youth to pay attention Volvo commissioned its touring car team, Polestar, to make a competition-inspired and fully functioning showcar. The results were truly amazing, with 400bhp and four-wheel drive enabling the C30 to hit 60mph in under five seconds. Sadly, the suits insist that this will remain a concept, but a rosy future, with Polestar doing for Volvo what M-Sport do for BMW, isn't out of the question.

2011 **Morgan 3-Wheeler** ▼

Bringing its pre-war glory days back to life, Morgan surprised the motoring world yet again in 2011 with the announcement that it was to start building its 3-Wheeler after a 70-odd year sabbatical.

Now equipped with an MX-5 gearbox and 2.0-litre, V-Twin, air-cooled engine from Harley Davison, you get modern-day reliability and modern-day performance, ensuring that the 3-Wheeler will be as impressively fast and involving as it is eccentric to the point of ridicule and totally impractical. Depending on your viewpoint, the £30,000 that Morgan want for it is either a bargain or burglary, but the world would be a poorer place without this sort of top-drawer madness.

29 April 2011

Prince William marries Kate Middleton to national jubilation, but the show is stolen by a blue Aston Martin DB6 Volante, which the happy couple use to drive down The Mall. The car was given to William's father, Prince Charles, as a 21st birthday present in 1969 and has been converted to run on bio-fuel produced from surplus English wine.

2011 **Aston Martin AMR-One** ▶

With class victories finally under its belt courtesy of the DBR9, a chipper Aston Martin turned its sights on the ultimate prize, an outright win at Le Mans. The car it scratch-built for the purpose was the AMR-One, an open cockpit racer that conformed to all the stringent new FIA regulations for the prototype class. This meant a modest, 2.0-litre, straight-six engine, but turbocharged to 540bhp and mated via a steel subframe to an all-carbon fibre chassis.

Just don't ask how the two works AMR-Ones faired in their Le Mans debut. (Six laps. Project cancelled. Shhh.)

2011 **Jaguar C-X75** ▲

Jaguar caught the world napping when it unveiled its mega-hybrid C-X75 concept. This was a proper futuristic fantasy, with twin gas-turbine engines and an electric motor for each wheel creating a four-wheel drive hypercar with a top speed in excess of 200mph, but emissions to rival a Toyota Prius. The shocks kept coming, too, when Jag's bosses announced that the C-X75 would go into limited series production in 2013. Although not entirely as technical as the original concept – the jet engines have to go – it will, nevertheless, be a visionary piece of engineering, finished with the help of the Williams F1 team who are tipped to supply a small but gigantically turbo'd four-cylinder engine and various elements of aerodynamic artistry.

2011 **Range Rover Evoque** ▼

Juggling attributes of coupé and SUV in a premium product at a competitive price, Range Rover took on a Herculean task when it drew up the Evoque. But it hit the mark, creating something practical and desirable, sporty and compact, as capable of heading off road as it is bouncing up the kerb outside the local nail salon. Although 'small' is a relative term when applied to the Range Rover brand, the Evoque is definitely closer to what the 21st-century demands of its SUVs. If this is the way the 4x4 is heading, we'll all be the better for it.

2011 **BMW 1-Series M** ▶

After ducking the issue for years, BMW finally unveiled the car we'd all be clamouring for. The 1-Series M, with its 335bhp, twin-turbo, 3.0-litre straight-six, is a hairy-chested handful in the old-school vein of agricultural grunt and rear-wheel drive. In an age where neutral handling and nanny state electronics are increasingly the norm, this is the spiritual successor to the original M3 and a shoo-in future classic.

2011 **BAC Mono** ▶

The single-seat BAC Mono is the latest in an increasingly illustrious line of hugely quick and hugely expensive track cars that bring the technology of serious racing to the road. With its central driving position, 280bhp, 2.3-litre Cosworth engine and sequential manual gearbox, the Mono provides outrageous levels of speed, adjustability and feedback for a car with a license plate. The catch is an £80k sticker price. Easy enough to justify for a formula racer on your driveway, less so to your other half who doesn't even get a seat.

2011 **Koenigsegg Agera** ▼

In the frozen Swedish hinterland, far away from the media frenzy around new Lambos and rocket-ship Bugattis, Koenigsegg has quietly built the other next big thing. The Agera is an all-carbon, twin-turbo V8, with 910bhp at the rear and no traction control. And for an extra £132,000 atop the £875,000 list price, the 'R' version will take it to 1115bhp. That's more than the Veyron SuperSport, in a car that weighs half a tonne less. Where's Chuck Yeager when you need him?

2011 **Lamborghini Sesto Elemento** ▼

The Sesto Elemento, the 'Sixth Element' on the periodic table, is carbon. And carbon fibre is what this car is all about. Eschewing power in favour of lightness, Lamborghini's visionary concept weighs in at 999kg, despite sharing the Gallardo's 5.2-litre V10 and four-wheel drive transmission. That's an astonishing 341kg less than even the lightweight Gallardo Superleggera.

A fully functioning car with a 0–60mph time of 2.5 seconds, the Sesto Elemento is, sadly, just a one-off, but it provides a tantalising peak at the engineering techniques and styling themes that will shape Lambo's future for years to come. It's all a far cry from Ferruccio's first tractor, all those years ago.

◄ 2011 **Porsche Cayman R**

As soon as the sub-911, mid-engined Cayman appeared, all people wanted to know was if Porsche were planning a 968-alike Clubsport version. 'Nein,' they said, before promptly unveiling the Cayman R.
Shedding 55kg, adding bucket seats, lowering the suspension, upping the power, this was the car Lotus, and 911 owners, were dreading. Focussed, purified Porsche perfection. Just don't call it a Clubsport.

2011 **Lamborghini Aventador** ▼

After a decade in the spotlight, the Murcielago breathed its last and Lamborghini began its top secret replacement. With a clean slate they could, and did, dial in anything and everything deemed necessary to make the ultimate modern supercar. The Aventador is a 700bhp monster with the world's first full carbon-fibre monocoque, F1-style pushrod suspension and an all-new 6.5-litre V12. Top speed is clocked at 217mph, but far more important is the handling – the best that Lamborghini has ever produced. Speed, presence and now topflight agility, all yours for a quarter mil.

2012 **Ferrari F12** ▶

For all Ferrari's acclaimed dabbling into ankle-biting mid-engined supercars and track-demolishing hyper-machinery, Maranello's heartland has always been gorgeous grand tourers with a giant V12 in the nose and a couple of well-heeled passengers clinging on behind. Enzo Ferrari himself, remember, always found the idea of sticking the engine behind the driver, rather than in front, a trifle vulgar. Even by Ferrari's stratospheric GT standards, the F12 is a bit special. Though smaller, lighter and more delicate than the 599 it replaces, the F12 is even quicker, its naturally aspirated 6.3-litre V12 kicking out a ridiculous 730bhp at a screaming 8000rpm. Bigger isn't always better.

2012 **Toyota GT86** ▼

Sometimes the old theories are the finest. Launched in early 2012, the GT86 – an identical twin of Subaru's BRZ – serves up not a new recipe but a classic one, cruelly neglected for a decade or two: lightweight, naturally aspirated engine up front, driven wheels at the rear, no-frills cabin in between. With just 200bhp from a 2.0-litre boxer engine, the GT86 will be outpaced by most diesel hatches, but with a skinny set of tyres (borrowed from a Prius, no less), it allows normal drivers a bit of tail-happy action at double-figure rather than triple-figure speeds. A car you can have fun in without approaching licence-losing velocity? Time to party like it's the early nineties...

2013 **Alfa Romeo 4C** ▶

Forget the Focus-rivalling hatchbacks and family estates: this is the stuff we want Alfa to do. Shown as a concept in 2011 and morphing into production guise two years later, the 4C is a gloriously extravagant, squat, two-seater coupé almost as wide as it is long. Though the mid-mounted engine is nothing more glamorous than a 1.7-litre, 237bhp turbo, the little Alfa makes the most of every one of its horsepowers by employing a featherweight carbon fibre monocoque, technology usually confined to the world of six-figure exotica rather than sub-£50,000 sports cars. It weighs less than a tonne. It's rear-drive. It has an Alfa badge and gorgeous 'cloverleaf' wheels. What more do you need?

2013 McLaren P1

One day, all this shall end. The car world's relentless, glorious pursuit of more power, more performance, more technology, more cool: whether through civil war, nuclear annihilation, the bloody uprising of the otters or, most likely, some pesky piece of government legislation banning all vehicles but Priuses and SsangYongs from public highways, eventually the fun will surely stop.

And, were the march of automotive progress to end tomorrow, the McLaren P1 would be a fitting epitaph to a century of cool cars. Arriving more than 20 years after McLaren's last hypercar – the epoch-defining, record-breaking, three-seat F1 – the P1 is as much of a game-changer as its illustrious forebear.

It is a hybrid, in pursuit not of economy and low emissions – though the P1's official mpg and CO_2 figures put some moderately frugal family cars to shame – but of ultimate acceleration. An electric motor, built with a helping hand from McLaren's F1 outfit, serves up 176bhp from a standstill, boosting low-end torque until the twin-turbo V8 engine deploys its full 727bhp at higher revs. All of which equals a combined power output of 903bhp and the sort of performance stats usually confined to surface-to-air missiles: 0-60mph takes less than three seconds, with a top speed of 218mph.

Despite its phenomenal power output, the P1 won't ever challenge the Veyron for the title of world's fastest production car. McLaren has said its aim wasn't to achieve the highest top speed in history, but to make the P1 the quickest, best-driving road car on a circuit. And that's what propels the P1 into proper *Tomorrow's World* territory: its mastery of the dark art of aerodynamics. A dizzying array of slats, flicks and vents – along with an enormous rear wing that lies dormant while accelerating but pops up to help with handling – provides a whopping 600kg of downforce, more than many Le Mans racers. And when you're done demolishing the motley array of Lamborghinis, Ferraris and Bugattis around the track, you can burble back to your palatial townhouse in spookily silent electric-only mode. Mr Jeckyll, meet Mr Hyde.

The cost, of course, is as stratospheric as the performance. Just 375 P1s will be built, costing just shy of £900,000. An absurd amount of money for four wheels and two seats? Or a cast-iron bargain for the most advanced slice of road-going technology on the planet? In truth, the P1 is both...

INDEX

CREDITS

P13, top: James Mann. *P13, centre:* Neill Bruce. *P17, top:* LAT; *bottom:* Magic Car Pics. *P19, top:* Tony Baker/Classic & Sports Car magazine. *P21, bottom:* James Mann. *P28:* Magic Car Pics. *P30, bottom:* Neill Bruce. *P39, top:* Zagato. *P41, top:* Karl Ludvigsen. *P43, top:* James Mann. *P51:* Magic Car Pics. *P53, bottom:* Magic Car Pics. *P63, top:* Alan Stote/Red Triangle. *P64, bottom:* Magic Car Pics. *P66, top:* James Mann; *bottom:* LAT. *P67, top:* Magic Car Pics. *P69, top:* BBC Top Gear magazine. *P72:* Magic Car Pics. *P74, centre:* Magic Car Pics. *P76-7:* Neill Bruce. *P78, bottom:* BBC Top Gear magazine. *P89, centre:* James Hale, author of The Dune Buggy Phenomenon. *P94, centre:* Kimballstock; *bottom:* Magic Car Pics. *P99, top:* LAT. *P104-5:* Magic Car Pics. *P107, top:* James Mann. *P111, bottom:* Magic Car Pics. *P113, bottom:* James Mann. *P115, top:* LAT; *bottom:* Kimballstock. *P116, top:* James Lipman/Classic & Sports Car magazine *P118: bottom:* Magic Car Pics. *P120:* Magic Car Pics. *P127, top:* Neill Bruce; *bottom:* Kimballstock. *P130, bottom:* Kimballstock. *P134, centre:* Magic Car Pics. *P137, bottom:* Coys. *P139, top:* LAT. *P151, bottom:* Magic Car Pics. *P154, bottom:* Magic Car Pics. *P157, top:* BBC Top Gear magazine. *P161:* Scott Schilke, SKS Racing. *P172, top:* Kobal.

P174: BBC Top Gear magazine. *P175, top:* James Mann. *P185, bottom:* LAT. *P186-7:* James Mann. *P193, bottom:* James Mann. *P197:* Motoring Picture Library, Beaulieu. *P199:* Magic Car Pics. *P205, top:* Neill Bruce. *P225, top:* BBC Top Gear magazine. *P228:* BBC Top Gear magazine. *P232, bottom;* BBC Top Gear magazine. *P237, bottom:* Andy Morgan/Evo/Dennis Publishing. *P254, bottom:* BBC Top Gear magazine. *P260, top:* BBC Top Gear magazine. *P266, top:* BBC Top Gear magazine. *P270, top:* BBC Top Gear magazine. *P280, bottom:* Autocar/LAT. *P291:* BBC Top Gear magazine. *P302:* BBC Top Gear magazine. *P304, bottom:* BBC Top Gear magazine.

All other images used in this book are from the Giles Chapman Library and/or the manufacturers concerned. Every effort has been made to credit, where necessary, the copyright holders of the images used, and BBC Books cannot be held responsible for any erroneous credits. However, amendments can be made to the picture acknowledgements in any future edition. We are particularly grateful to the many photographers working for BBC Top Gear magazine, whose images appear in this book by permission of the magazine's editorial department.

10 9 8 7 6 5 4 3 2 1

First published in 2012 by BBC Books, an imprint of Ebury Publishing.
A Random House Group company.

This updated edition published in 2013.

Main text by Matt Master
Copyright © Woodlands Books Ltd 2012

Top Gear (word marks and logos) is a trademark of the British Broadcasting Corporation and used under licence.
Top Gear © 2005

The Random House Group Limited Reg. 954009

Addresses for companies within the Random House Group can be found at www.randomhouse.co.uk

A CIP catalogue record for this book is available from the British Library.

ISBN 978 1 84 990633 3

The Random House Group Limited supports the Forest Stewardship Council® (FSC®), the leading international forest-certification organisation. Our books carrying the FSC label are printed on FSC®-certified paper. FSC is the only forest-certification scheme supported by the leading environmental organisations, including Greenpeace. Our paper procurement policy can be found at www.randomhouse.co.uk/environment

Commissioning Editor: **Lorna Russell**
In-house Editor: **Joe Cottington**
Project Editor: **Rod Green**
Design: **Method UK**
Picture Researcher: **Giles Chapman**

Printed and bound in China by C&C Offset Printing Co., Ltd

To buy books by your favourite authors and register for offers, visit www.randomhouse.co.uk